Cultural Explorations

Multicultural Readings
with Integrated Language Skills

Jeanne B. Becijos

Dominie Press, Inc.

Copyright © 2004 Dominie Press, Inc.
All rights reserved. No part of this publication may be reproduced or transmitted in any form or by any means without permission in writing from the publisher. Reproduction of any part of this book, through photocopy, recording, or any electronic or mechanical retrieval system, without the written permission of the publisher, is an infringement of the copyright law.

Published by:

Dominie Press, Inc.

1949 Kellogg Avenue
Carlsbad, California 92008 USA

ISBN 0-7685-0178-4
Printed in Singapore by PH Productions Pte Ltd

1 2 3 4 5 6 PH 05 04 03

Contents

Introduction to the Teacher — v-vi

Scope and Sequence — vii-viii

Unit 1
The Butchart Gardens – Canada — 1

Unit 2
Sculptures in Stone – Zimbabwe — 9

Unit 3
The Festival of Loi Krathong – Thailand — 16

Unit 4
The Boy Who Took Care of Pigs – Mexico — 23

Unit 5
Basanth—the First Day of Spring – Pakistan — 30

Unit 6
The Gauchos – Argentina — 38

Unit 7
The Mouse Bride – Finland — 46

Unit 8
The Lion and the Hare – Iran — 53

Unit 9
Manatees – Cuba — 60

Unit 10
Three Major Cities – the United States — 67

Contents

Unit 11
The Sahara Desert – Algeria …… 74

Unit 12
The Snow Woman – Japan …… 81

Unit 13
Pablo Picasso – Spain …… 88

Unit 14
The Widow and the Fish – Indonesia …… 95

Unit 15
Helen Keller – the United States …… 102

Unit 16
Travels in Laos – Laos …… 109

Unit 17
The Panama Canal – Panama …… 116

Unit 18
Life in Antarctica – Antarctica …… 122

Unit 19
Nzinga, Queen of Ndongo and Matamba – Angola …… 129

Unit 20
The Pot of Gold – Moldova …… 136

Introduction to the Teacher

Cultural Explorations is a multicultural reader with language exercises. The reading material contains biographies, holidays, folk tales, and descriptions of people and places from representative areas around the world. The readings and exercises are appropriate for ESL/ELD and bilingual students in elementary grades, junior high, high school, and adult basic education.

The text provides interesting and motivating reading for ESL/ELD students at the intermediate language level in English.

Each unit begins with questions that introduce the country involved and the topic of the reading. The reading selection is followed by listening, speaking, grammar, and writing exercises that relate to the topic. The units may be completed in a different sequence, as needed, and done in class with teacher assistance. Some sections of the unit such as Grammar Practice, Language Practice, Check Your Understanding, Check Your Progress, and Writing for Your Portfolio might be assigned as homework.

The listening and speaking activities in each unit give students practice with communication skills. The value of learning grammar and language is to assist students with comprehension of their reading and to provide them with rules to correct their writing. As the grammar and language are presented in context, the students see language as it occurs naturally.

All of these skills are valuable in preparing students for advanced academic courses. While the students are improving their language skills, they are also learning valuable information about people and countries from across the globe.

To facilitate instruction using *Cultural Explorations*, use the following information and teaching suggestions.

Introduction

Each unit is introduced by questions regarding the geographic location of the country referred to in the reading and listening selections. These questions include naming the continent and bordering countries. You can point out each country on a globe or large map with the whole class. You may wish to review the continents and major countries with the class before you start the book. In this section, there are also true/false statements that activate students' prior knowledge regarding the country. The third question allows students to make a personal connection to the upcoming reading topic. Directly prior to the reading section, there is a question related to the theme or a main concept of the reading. This prereading question will help focus the students on comprehension of the main idea.

Reading Selection and Questions

The reading selections include biographies, holidays, folk tales, and descriptions of people and places from representative areas around the world. You or a student may choose to read the selection aloud, or you may ask the students to read the selection silently and answer the questions independently, with a partner, or in a small group. Each reading selection is followed by a glossary of challenging key terms. Students may answer the questions in the Comprehension Check exercise either orally with the class or in writing.

Listening

This section begins with a prelistening exercise to introduce vocabulary and concepts. The prelistening exercise is followed by a listening exercise about the listening selection, which the teacher reads aloud from the listening script at the end of the book. The listening exercises cover a variety of skills, such as listening to questions, chart completion, charting facts, and listening for information. Students complete the activity as described in the listening exercise. A follow-up exercise, postlistening, is a reflection or personalized commentary in response to the topic of the listening exercise.

Grammar Exercise

The grammar section explains various points of grammar that are utilized within each unit. These exercises practice the grammar points and review the information learned at the same time. You may introduce the grammar on the board, along with additional examples, to further clarify the lesson. Students may answer the questions independently, with a partner, or in a small group.

Speaking

This activity follows the grammar section and offers students an opportunity to speak with a partner. Students work in pairs, asking and answering the questions listed. These questions are related to the unit topic and utilize the grammar points found in the unit, giving students the chance to use the structures.

Language

This section provides explanations and practice on topics such as capitalization, punctuation, spelling rules, vocabulary, and other information related to learning a language. You may want to give additional examples on the board. The items in the practice exercise are again related to the unit topic. Students can answer the questions independently, with a partner, or in a small group.

Check Your Understanding

This section offers additional practice on the language topic from the language section. Students can demonstrate their ability to independently apply the language lesson. Students may complete the activity independently, with a partner, or in a small group.

Check Your Progress

To further check students' knowledge of the grammar and language information, students correct a paragraph with errors. The errors relate to the grammar and language from the unit, include misspelled words, and refer to grammar and language points from prior units. You may want to do a sample line from the paragraph together as a class. You may even choose to do the entire paragraph with the class, as students write the correct answers on their papers.

Writing for Your Portfolio

In a final demonstration of language competency, students have the opportunity to write a paragraph utilizing the grammar point from the unit. Students are given guide questions and are told to follow the format of the sample paragraph. You may also lead the students in further brainstorming and/or sharing of ideas with a partner before writing the paragraph. After completing the paragraph, you may want to have students trade papers and make responses on content. The students may choose to polish the writing and maintain a final copy in a portfolio.

Scope and Sequence

Unit	Listening	Grammar	Language	Writing
1	Listening for words to complete a dialog	Present Tense 'to be'	Punctuation Rules: End Marks	Description of a place
2	Listening for information that is true or false	Simple Present Tense Statements	Punctuation: Commas with Words in a Series	Directions on how to make something
3	Listening for specific information to answer questions	Simple Present Tense Questions	Rules for Capitalization	Questions and answers about a holiday
4	Listening to respond to specific questions	Simple Past Tense: Irregular Verbs	Sentence Fragments	Short Story
5	Listening for and matching information	Present Continuous Tense	Run-on Sentences	Descriptive paragraph on activities
6	Listening for specific information about a story	Count and Non-count Nouns	Spelling Rules: Plural Nouns	Informative paragraph about a country
7	Listening to respond to specific questions	Past Continuous Tense	Prepositions of Time	Autobiography
8	Listening to identify characters in a story	Reflexive Pronouns	Spelling Rules: Using 'i' and 'e' Together	Description of activities
9	Listening for information that is true or false	Comparative Form of Adjectives	Punctuation: colon	Business letter to request information
10	Listening to differentiate opinions	Superlative Form of Adjectives	Spelling Rules: Doubling Final Consonants	Comparison of three places
11	Listening for specific words to complete a paragraph	Indefinite Pronouns	Vocabulary: Antonyms	Summary of a survey

Scope and Sequence

Unit	Listening	Grammar	Language	Writing
12	Listening to respond to specific questions	Modals: 'should,' 'have to,' 'must'	Parts of Speech: Nouns, Pronouns, and Verbs	Giving advice
13	Listening to match terms with definitions	Modals: 'may,' 'might,' and 'could'	Parts of Speech: Adjectives, Prepositions, and Conjunctions	Description of a place
14	Listening for percentages	Adjectives and Adverbs	Vocabulary: Antonyms	Description of an accomplishment
15	Listening for information that is true or false	Indirect Objects	Suffixes: '-ful' and '-less'	Description of challenge
16	Listening to match topics with descriptions	Present Perfect Tense	Confusing Words: 'it's' and 'its'	Friendly letter
17	Listening to distinguish between true and false statements	Gerunds	Abbreviations	Description of weekend activities
18	Listening for specific information to complete a chart	Passive Voice: Simple Present Tense	Vocabulary: Words from Science	Research and write about an animal
19	Listening for facts to fill in blanks in an outline	Passive Voice: Simple Past Tense	Confusing words: 'then' and 'than'	Biography
20	Listening to respond to specific questions	Reported Speech	Punctuation: Quotation Marks	Writing & Conversation

Unit 1

The Butchart Gardens

A. INTRODUCTION

1. On which continent is Canada? Name the country that borders on Canada.

2. Which two of the following statements are true about Canada?
    a. Canada is the second largest nation in the world in area.
    b. The major languages in Canada are English and French.
    c. The land in Canada is mostly deserts with no forests.

3. Do you like gardens? Why or why not?

UNIT 1

B. READING ACTIVITY

The Butchart Gardens in Canada are some of the most beautiful gardens in the world.

1. Reading Selection: The Butchart Gardens

Canada is a beautiful country. There are many places to visit. One famous place is the Butchart Gardens. These beautiful gardens are in the southwest part of Canada on Vancouver Island. The place isn't hard to find. The gardens are 13 miles north of the city of Victoria in British Columbia.

The Butchart Gardens are very large and very popular. They are on 50 acres of land. The gardens are open every day, even on holidays. Nearly 1,000,000 people visit the gardens each year. People visit the gardens from all over the world. There are audio guides to the gardens in 18 languages. People in wheelchairs can also tour the Butchart Gardens. The weather is nice most of the year. It isn't as cold as most of Canada.

The Butchart and Ross families run the gardens. In 1904, Mr. and Mrs. Robert Butchart started the gardens at their home. The Butcharts loved to travel. The flowers and trees in their gardens are from all over the world. Today 50 gardeners work in the gardens. They put in 1,000,000 plants a year. The gardens have different names. Some of the names are the Rose Garden, the Italian Garden, the Japanese Garden, and the Sunken Garden. There are different kinds of flowers all year long. In the winter there is holly. In the summer you see roses everywhere.

Summers are special in the Butchart Gardens. The gardens are open in the evening from June to September. The gardens and water areas have lights. In summer there are also fireworks on Saturday evenings.

Glossary

| Fireworks | Holly | Wheelchair |

2. Comprehension Check

Answer the following questions about the reading selection.

a. Where are the Butchart Gardens?

b. When are the Butchart Gardens open?

c. Would you like to visit the Butchart Gardens? Why or why not?

C. LISTENING ACTIVITY

1. **Prelistening**
   Listen quietly as your teacher reads the story again about the Butchart Gardens. Imagine you are in the garden. How do you feel?

2. **Listening**
   First, look up the meaning of the words below that you do not know. Next, listen to the conversation about the Butchart Gardens. Complete the sentences in the conversation. Choose from the words in the box below to complete the sentences.

spring	summer	fall	winter	interested	see
visit	roses	holly	with	fireworks	special
sure	beautiful	lovely	aren't	isn't	hours

   Mike: What is your favorite place to _____ ?
   a

   Brandi: I love to visit the Butchart Gardens. That place is just _____ !
   b

   Mike: Is it far?

   Brandi: No. The gardens _____ very far. They are four _____ from my house.
   c   d

   Mike: When do you go?

   Brandi: I go all year long. There are cherry trees and daisies in the_____ . In the
   e
   summer there are _____ . Also at night there are _____ . In the_____
   f   g   h
   I like the colors of the trees. At Christmas time there are_____ lights and music.
   i

   Mike: Hey, now I'm _____ in the gardens. Can I go_____ you some time?
   j   k

   Brandi: _____ !
   l

3. **Postlistening**
   After listening to the conversation, talk about when you would like to go to the gardens. Would you like to go in the summer? At night? At Christmas time?

UNIT 1

3

UNIT 1

D. GRAMMAR: Present Tense "to be"

1. Grammar Explanation

Study the information and examples below.

Present Tense: Statements with "to be"			
	I	am (am not)	happy.
	You We They	are (aren't)	happy.
	The gardens	are (aren't)	beautiful.
	He She It	is (isn't)	famous.

Present Tense: Questions with "to be"			
Am	I		happy?
Are	you we they		happy?
Are	the gardens		beautiful?
Is	he she it		famous?

2. Grammar Practice

First choose the verb to make the sentence *correct*. Then rewrite each sentence.

Example: Canada (is) (isn't) a beautiful country.
Canada *is* a beautiful country.

a. There (are) (aren't) many places to see in Canada.
___

b. The Butchart Gardens (are) (aren't) in the northwest part of Canada.
___

c. Visitors (are) (aren't) welcome to the Butchart Gardens.
___

d. The Butchart Gardens (are) (aren't) closed on holidays.
___

e. The weather (is) (isn't) nice in the Butchart Gardens area.
___

f. There (are) (aren't) audio guides for the Butchart Gardens in 50 languages.
___

g. There (is) (isn't) holly in the gardens in the winter.
___

E. SPEAKING

Ask a partner the following questions. Then change roles.

1. What are your favorite places to see around here?
2. When do you visit those places?
3. What are your favorite flowers or trees?
4. Do you plant flowers or trees? Why or why not?
5. Are summers special to you? Why or why not?

F. LANGUAGE: Punctuation Rules - End Marks

1. Language Explanation

Read the information about punctuation rules for endmarks below.

Punctuation Rules: End Marks		
1. Period (.) Use a period at the end of the sentence **Example:** *Visitors are welcome.*	**2. Question Mark (?)** Use a question mark at the end of a question. **Example:** *Is it far?*	**3. Exclamation Point (!)** Use an exclamation point to add emphasis or to show emotion. **Example**: *The Butchart Gardens are just beautiful!*

2. Language Practice

First use the correct end mark. Then rewrite the sentences.

Example: Are there roses in the city ___
Are there roses in the city?

a. The weather is nice all year long ___

b. The Butchart Gardens are very large ___

c. Where are the Butchart Gardens ___

d. The fireworks are great ___

e. The gardens have flowers from all over the world ___

f. Sure ___

g. Why are there 50 gardeners ___

h. The gardens are open in the summer evenings ___

G. CHECK YOUR UNDERSTANDING

Finish writing this conversation. Add four more lines. Use three different end marks in your conversation.

Dave: What time is it?

Jan: It's 11:00.

Dave: Oh, I'm late!

Jan: Where are you going?

Dave:

Jan:

Dave:

Jan:

H. CHECK YOUR PROGRESS

Rewrite the paragraph below and correct the errors. Look for two verb errors, one spelling error, and two end mark errors. There is *one* error in each sentence.

> Restaurants is popular in the Butchart Gardens. Some people eat lunch or dinner! Others have afternoon tea? There are also music at the gardens. The Butchart Gardens are really beautiful.

Example: Restaurants *are* popular in the Butchart Gardens.

___
___
___
___
___
___
___

7

UNIT 1

I. WRITING FOR YOUR PORTFOLIO

Write a paragraph about a place you like to visit.

Example: The British Columbia Provincial Museum

I like to visit the British Columbia Provincial Museum. It is in the city of Victoria in Canada. Everyone can go to this museum. You can go to visit the museum during the day. I like the museum because there are exhibits about the native people and the history of the area.

Your Paragraph:

Here are some guide questions.

What is the place?
Where is the place?
Who can go to the place?
When can you go to the place?
Why do you like the place?

_____

_____

_____

_____

_____

_____

Unit 2

Sculptures in Stone

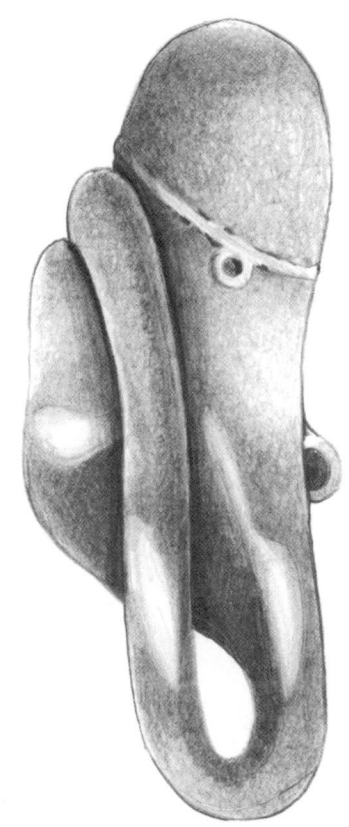

A. INTRODUCTION

1. On which continent is Zimbabwe? Name two countries that border on Zimbabwe.

2. Which two of the following statements are true about Zimbabwe?
   a. Zimbabwe is the largest country in Africa.
   b. There are wonderful artists in Zimbabwe.
   c. Zimbabwe has animals such as hippopotamuses, giraffes, and elephants.

3. Do you know how to make sculptures? What material do you use?

UNIT 2

B. READING ACTIVITY

This reading tells of the Zimbabwe people's beautiful work with sculptures.

1. Reading Selection: Sculptures in Stone

The Zimbabwe people are famous for their stone sculptures. These sculptures are sold all over the world. Many of the sculptures look like modern art.

Most of the artists learn from other sculptors. They usually don't learn from schools about their art. Most of the sculptors are men. There are some women sculptors, though. Almost all the sculptors are Shona people. These people first came to Zimbabwe about 1,500 years ago.

It takes a long time to make a sculpture. First, the artist finds a raw stone. Then, he begins to hit the stone with a hammer and chisel. He carves the details. He then uses water and sand to smooth the stone. Next, he puts the stone in the fire. Finally he puts a wax coat on the stone. The wax shows the beautiful colors of the stone. There are various colors, such as black, red, or green. The process takes weeks or months to finish.

Many of the artists make sculptures of animals and nature. Some of the sculptures represent spirits. The early Shona people spoke of the spirits in animals and nature. For example, the elephant represents the spirit of patience and long life. The Shona respect the elephants for being loyal. Elephants help one another. Family loyalty is very important with the people in Zimbabwe today. The artists also make sculptures of lions, birds, and hippos.

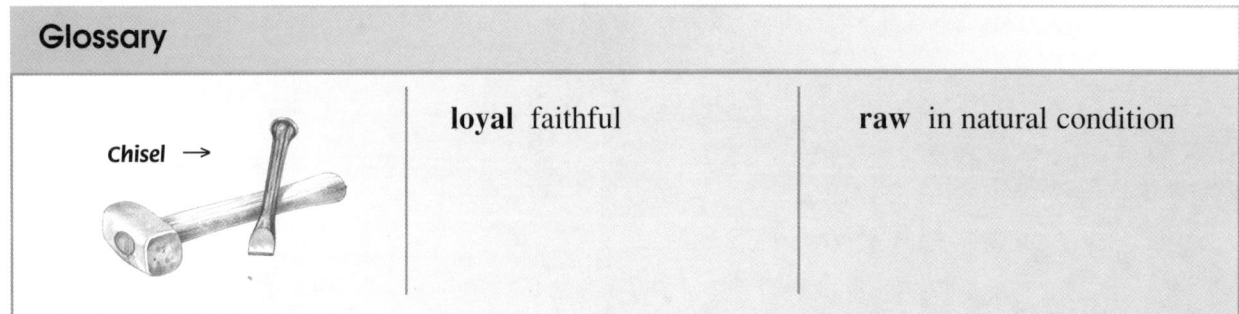

Glossary

Chisel →

loyal faithful

raw in natural condition

2. Comprehension Check
Answer the following questions about the reading selection.

a. What is one reason Zimbabwe people are famous?

b. How long does it take to make a stone sculpture?

c. How much do you think Zimbabwe sculptures cost?

C. LISTENING ACTIVITY

1. **Prelistening**

   When you think of art, what do you think of? Paintings? Sculptures? Drawings? Which is your favorite kind of art and why?

2. **Listening**

   Listen to the selection about Shona sculptures from Zimbabwe. Listen for the following information:

   - what the Shona people are famous for
   - when early Shona sculpture started
   - what the Shona people made
   - where you can find stone bird

   Now, mark the following sentences true (**T**) or false (**F**) according to the information from the listening selection.

		T	F
a.	In Zimbabwe, the Shona people are famous for their sculptures.	__	__
b.	In Zimbabwe, the Shona people are famous for their elephants.	__	__
c.	For the Shona people, sculpture started 50 years ago.	__	__
d.	Sculpture started long ago for the Shona people.	__	__
e.	These people made sculptures 1,000 years ago.	__	__
f.	The Shona made birds from red stone.	__	__
g.	The Shona made birds from green stone for their building tops.	__	__
h.	You can find the stone birds in a museum in Zimbabwe.	__	__

3. **Postlistening**

   What would you be most interested in seeing?
   Recent Shona sculptures?
   Older Shona sculptures?
   The museum?

UNIT 2

D. GRAMMAR

1. Grammar Explanation
Study the information and examples below.

Use "he," "she," "it," and singular nouns with the third person singular verb.
Add '-s' to the verb to form the third person singular verb.

Simple Present Tense Statements: Third Person Singular

SUBJECT	VERB + 's'	
The artist	finds	a raw stone.
He	carves	the details.
She	puts	the stone in the fire.
The elephant	represents	the spirit of patience.

Other Forms of the Simple Present Tense

SUBJECT	VERB	
I	like	sculptures.
You	see	sculptures in a museum.
They	make	sculptures.
Many people	buy	Shona sculptures.

2. Grammar Practice
First choose the correct verb. Then rewrite the following sentences as true or false, according to the selection.

Example: The artists (learns) (learn) from other sculptors.
           The artists *learn* from other sculptors.

a. The artists in Zimbabwe usually (goes) (go) to art schools.

    _____ ( )

b. The Zimbabwe sculptures (looks) (look) like modern art.

    _____ ( )

c. First the artist (finds) (find) a raw stone.

    _____ ( )

d. He (hits) (hit) the stone with a hammer and stone.

_____ (   )

e. The artist (uses) (use) water and sand to smooth the stone.

_____ (   )

f. He (puts) (put) the stone in the fire.

_____ (   )

g. The artist (takes) (take) days to finish the sculpture.

_____ (   )

h. The elephant (represents) (represent) patience and long life.

_____ (   )

E. SPEAKING

Ask a partner the following questions. Then change roles.

1. What does a Shona artist make?
2. How long does it take?
3. What does a sculptor use in his work?
4. What does a dancer do?
5. What does an artist want?

F. LANGUAGE

1. **Language Explanation**
   Read the information about using commas with words in a series below.

   > **Punctuation: Commas with Words in a Series**
   >
   > Use commas to separate words in a series.
   >
   > **Examples:**
   > *The artists make sculptures of lions, birds, and hippopotamuses.*
   > *The sculptors use black, red, or green colors.*

UNIT 2

2. Language Practice

First add commas to separate words in a series. Then rewrite each sentence.

> **Example:** The sculpture takes weeks months or years to finish.
> *The sculpture takes weeks, months, or years to finish.*

a. The main languages in Zimbabwe are English Shona and Sindebele.
___

b. Zambia South Africa and Mozambique border on Zimbabwe.
___

c. Zimbabwe mines gold copper and nickel.
___

d. The biggest cities in Zimbabwe are Harare Bulawayo and Chitungwiza.
___

e. Zimbabwe exports cotton tobacco and cattle.
___

f. The colors of the flag of Zimbabwe are green yellow red black and white.
___

G. CHECK YOUR UNDERSTANDING

Write four sentences with facts about your country. Use the sentences above with information about Zimbabwe as examples.

1. ___
2. ___
3. ___
4. ___

H. CHECK YOUR PROGRESS

Rewrite the paragraph below and correct the errors. Look for three present tense verb errors and two comma errors. There is *one* error in each sentence.

> The Shona artist make sculptures of animals. The Shona believe, that animals have different qualities. The elephant is patient loyal, and helpful. The lion represent order and tradition. The giraffe like to know about everything.

Example: The Shona artist *makes* sculptures of animals.

I. WRITING FOR YOUR PORTFOLIO

Write about how to make something. Use words like "first," "then," "next," and "finally" in your directions. Use a comma after these words at the beginning of the sentence.

Example: How to Make a Sculpture

First, the artist finds a raw stone. Then he begins to hit the stone with a hammer and chisel. He carves the details. He then uses water and sand to smooth the stone. Next, he puts the stone in the fire. Finally, he puts a wax coat on the stone.

Your Paragraph:

Unit 3

The Festival of Loi Krathong

A. INTRODUCTION

1. On which continent is Thailand? Name two countries that border on Thailand.

2. Which two of the following statements do you think are true about Thailand?
   a. The capital of Thailand is Moscow.
   b. Thailand is one of the world's leading exporters of rice.
   c. More than 95% of Thais are Buddhist in religion.

3. What do people do during festivals?

B. READING ACTIVITY

The festival of Loi Krathong in Thailand is a time to show respect for nature.

1. Reading Selection: The Festival of Loi Krathong

Mark is visiting the home of Pani in Thailand. It is the time of Loi Krathong, a special festival. This festival occurs on the day of the full moon at the end of the rainy season. It is usually in November.

Pani: I'm glad you're visiting us now. You can see the festival of Loi Krathong.

Mark: Why do you celebrate Loi Krathong?

Pani: We want to show our respect. We give thanks to the spirit of rivers.

Mark: Is this a religious holiday? Do you celebrate Buddhism with Loi Krathong?

Pani: No, this festival began long ago. It started before Buddhism. Then the people believed in the spirits of nature. Rivers, animals, and trees all had spirits. People respected these spirits. Today we still show respect for nature.

Mark: What does Krathong mean in your language?

Pani: Krathongs are the lanterns for the water. We make lanterns from banana leaves. The lanterns look like lotus flowers. We put a candle, flowers, and coins in the Krathongs. At night we get near the water. Then we put the Krathongs in the water. We make a wish. We want our mistakes to disappear with the river.

Mark: Do you have fun on this holiday?

Pani: Oh, yes! The festival starts in the morning. We have a parade. The people dress in special clothes. Children carry Krathongs in the parade. Water buffaloes and elephants are also in the parade. At night there are fireworks and dances.

Mark: I know I'll enjoy this holiday.

Glossary

Buddhism a religion from Asia   **lantern** object to enclose a light
water buffalo a buffalo from the old world with wide curving horns

2. Comprehension Check

Answer the following questions about the reading selection.

a. What country is Mark visiting?
b. What is the special festival they are celebrating?
c. When did this festival begin?
d. When do they celebrate Krathong?
e. Is it a religious celebration?
f. What is Krathong?
g. Do you like festivals? Why or why not?

UNIT 3

C. LISTENING ACTIVITY

1. Prelistening
You are going to discover some information about Thailand. Listen for the facts below:

- the age children go to school
- how many televisions and telephones there are per person
- how long men and women are expected to live

2. Listening
First read the following questions. Then listen to information for the answers and write the answers.

a. What are the ages when children must go to school?
b. How many televisions are there per person in Thailand?
c. How many telephones are there per person in Thailand?
d. How long are men expected to live in Thailand?
e. How long are women expected to live in Thailand?

3. Postlistening
Talk about the information about Thailand and compare it to the United States. Do children have to go to school in the United States? At what age can children quit school in the United States? Do you think that everyone in the United States has a TV? Who lives longer in the U.S., men or women?

D. GRAMMAR: Simple Present Tense Statements

1. Grammar Explanation
Study the information and examples below.

Use "do" with "I," "you," and "they."
Use "does" with "he," "she," and "it."
Use these words to ask questions: "what," "where," "when," "how," and "why."

Simple Present Tense Questions				
	Do	you	have	fun on this holiday?
	Does	everyone	have	a television?
Why	do	they	celebrate	Krathong?
What	does	Krathong	mean?	
Where	do	people	have	a parade?

18

2. Grammar Practice

First use the correct verb and rewrite the questions.
Then circle "yes" or "no," according to the reading.

Example: (Do) (Does) Pani live in Thailand? Yes [x] No ☐
Does Pani live in Thailand?

a. (Do) (Does) Pani like the festival of Loi Krathong? Yes ☐ No ☐

_____

b. (Do) (Does) Loi Krathong occur in September? Yes ☐ No ☐

_____

c. (Do) (Does) people celebrate Buddhism with Loi Krathong? Yes ☐ No ☐

_____

d. (Do) (Does) the Thais respect nature? Yes ☐ No ☐

_____

e. (Do) (Does) Krathong mean river? Yes ☐ No ☐

_____

f. (Do) (Does) the Thais make lanterns from banana leaves? Yes ☐ No ☐

_____

g. (Do) (Does) the Thais have a parade for Loi Krathong? Yes ☐ No ☐

_____

h. (Do) (Does) everyone in the world celebrate Loi Krathong? Yes ☐ No ☐

_____

E. SPEAKING

Ask a partner the following questions. Then change roles.

1. Do you like parades?
2. Where do you see parades?
3. When do you see parades?
4. Why do/don't you like parades?
5. When is the last time you went to a parade?

UNIT 3

F. LANGUAGE: Rules of Capitalization

1. Language Explanation
Read the information about rules of capitalization below.

Rules of Capitalization

Use a capital letter:
1. at the beginning of a sentence
   Example: *We make a wish.*
2. for the pronoun "I"
   Example: *I like this festival.*
3. for all the names of persons, places, or things
   Examples: *Pani   Mark   Thais   Thailand   Bangkok   Buddhism*
4. for days of the week, months, and holidays
   Examples:
   Monday   January   Loi Krathong
   Tuesday   November   New Year's Day

2. Language Practice
Use capital letters correctly and rewrite these sentences.

Example: they believe in buddhism. *They* believe in *Buddhism.*

a. mark is visiting pani in thailand.

b. the festival of loi krathong occurs usually during november.

c. loi krathong is not a buddhist holiday.

d. i like the parades in the city of bangkok.

e. new year's day is the first day of january.

f. i think new year's day is on a monday this year.

g. christmas is a popular holiday in the united states.

h. monday, tuesday, wednesday, thursday, friday, saturday, and sunday are the days of the week.

G. CHECK YOUR UNDERSTANDING

In four separate sentences, write the names of four holidays and the month in which they occur.

Example: *Christmas is in December.*

1. _____
2. _____
3. _____
4. _____

H. CHECK YOUR PROGRESS

Rewrite the paragraph below and correct the errors. Look for one verb error, one spelling error, and three capitalization errors. There is *one* error in each sentence.

> Does you know the country of Thailand? It is in asia. Thailand is in the shape of an elephant's head. many people like to visit Thailand. A good time to visit is in november.

Example: *Do* you know the country of Thailand?

_____
_____
_____
_____

UNIT 3

I. WRITING FOR YOUR PORTFOLIO

Write four questions and four answers about a holiday or festival you know about.

Examples:

1. What holiday do you like?
I like the Thai New Year. It is called Songkran.

2. When do you celebrate New Year's?
We celebrate New Year's in April.

3. What do you do on this holiday?
We pour water on the statues and pictures of Buddha. We also pour scented water on each other. It is the hottest time of year. It's also a time for enjoying all the foods the season has to offer.

4. Does everyone celebrate this day? Yes, almost everyone celebrates Songkran. It's lots of fun.

Your Questions

1. Question: _____

Answer: _____

2. Question: _____

Answer: _____

3. Question: _____

Answer: _____

4. Question: _____

Answer: _____

Unit 4

The Boy Who Took Care of Pigs

A. INTRODUCTION

1. On which continent is Mexico? Name two countries that border on Mexico.

2. Which two of the following statements are true about Mexico?
   a. Many ancient people had early civilizations in Mexico.
   b. Mexico's land includes deserts, mountains, and tropical areas.
   c. Antarctica ruled Mexico for a few years during the 1800s.

3. The story, "The Boy Who Took Care of Pigs," is about a boy who found something special. Did you ever find something valuable? What was it?

UNIT 4

B. READING ACTIVITY

This Mexican story is about a boy trying to help his family.

1. Reading Selection: The Boy Who Took Care of Pigs

Juanito was six years old. He lived with his mother and father in a mud house. They were very poor. The father was sick. He couldn't work. Juanito took care of pigs for a rich man.

Every day Juanito took the pigs to the woods. The pigs looked for food in the woods. Juanito found wood. He took the wood home for his family. One day the pigs were digging for food. They found some special wood. It was very heavy. The boy took the wood home.

"Juanito, where did you get this wood?" asked Juanito's father.
"The pigs dug it out of the ground," answered Juanito.
"These are special sticks. We will save them." The father put them around the room.

Every day the boy brought home more sticks of the special wood. The father had an idea about the special wood. The wood was really sticks of silver. Maybe some bandits left the silver in the woods. But the father didn't tell Juanito about his idea.

After ten years, the rich man moved away. He sold all his pigs.

"Father, I don't have a job. What can we do?" Juanito asked sadly.

His father said, "We'll use the sticks." They took some of the sticks to the government. The government gave them a sack of money in return. "Look! Now we are rich!" said the father.

Juanito and his parents built a beautiful house. They had roses and trees around the house. They had silver dishes and fine food. Every night they invited the poorest people in town to eat with them. Juanito and his parents were happy indeed.

Glossary	
bandit robber	**take care of** watch; give food to

2. Comprehension Check
Answer the following questions about the reading selection.

   a. What is Juanito's job?

   b. What does Juanito find in the woods?

   c. What do Juanito and his parents do with the money?

C. LISTENING ACTIVITY

1. **Prelistening**

   In the story, the boy took home something valuable. What things are valuable to you? What do you do with valuable things? If you find something valuable, what will you do?

2. **Listening**

   First listen to the story as your teacher reads it out loud. Then listen to your teacher read some questions about the story. Write the answers to the questions you hear.

   a. _____

   b. _____

   c. _____

   d. _____

   e. _____

   f. _____

   g. _____

   h. _____

   i. _____

   j. _____

3. **Postlistening**

   An important idea of this story is sharing your wealth with others. Do you like to help others in need? How do you help them?

D. GRAMMAR: Simple Past Tense - Irregular Verbs

1. **Grammar Explanation**
   Study the information and examples below.

   ### Simple Past Tense - Irregular Verbs

   Many verbs we use frequently have special past tense forms.

PRESENT	PAST	PRESENT	PAST
(be) am, is, are	was, were	leave	left
bring	brought	put	put
build	built	say	said
dig	dug	see	saw
find	found	sell	sold
give	gave	take	took
have	had		

   Examples: *Juanito and his parents* **built** *a beautiful house.*
   Juanito and his parents **were** *happy.*

2. **Grammar Practice**
   First change the verbs in parentheses ( ) from present tense to past tense. Then, mark the sentences true (T) or false (F) according to the information from the reading selection.

   Example: Juanito and his parents (are) poor.
   Juanito and his parents *were* poor. **(True)**

	T	F

   1. Juanito (is) four years old in the story. ____ ____

   2. Every day Juanito (takes) the pigs to the woods. ____ ____

   3. The pigs (find) some special food. ____ ____

   4. The father (puts) the sticks in the yard. ____ ____

   5. Some bandits (leave) the silver at Juanito's house. ____ ____

   6. The rich man (sells) all of his pigs after 10 years. ____ ____

   7. The government (gives) the family sticks in return. ____ ____

   8. Juanito and his parents (build) a beautiful house. ____ ____

E. SPEAKING

Ask a partner the following questions. Then change roles.

1. Where did you put your shoes last night?
2. What did you give your sister for her birthday last year?
3. When did you leave your house this morning?
4. What did your friend say to you on the phone last week?
5. What did the teacher bring to class yesterday?

F. LANGUAGE

1. **Language Explanation**

   Read the information about sentence fragments below.

   > **Sentence Fragments**
   >
   > A complete sentence has a subject and a predicate. A sentence fragment is an incomplete sentence. A fragment usually has a subject or a predicate missing.

   Examples:

Sentence Fragment	Complete Sentence
Out of the ground.	*The pig dug it out of the ground.*
Were very poor.	*They were very poor.*
Juanito six years old.	*Juanito was six years old.*
Really sticks of silver.	*The wood was really sticks of silver.*

2. **Language Practice**

   Read the following sentences and decide if they are complete sentences or sentence fragments. Check "cs" or "sf" after each sentence.

   Examples: Some of the sticks.   *sentence fragment*
   The father put some of the sticks down.   *complete sentence*

		cs	sf
a.	Juanito lived with his parents.	___	___
b.	In a mud house.	___	___
c.	They were very poor.	___	___
d.	Juanito took care of pigs.	___	___
e.	For a rich man.	___	___
f.	The pigs to the woods.	___	___
g.	Was very heavy.	___	___
h.	Some bandits in the woods.	___	___
i.	They took the sticks to the government.	___	___
j.	Every night they invited the poorest people.	___	___

UNIT 4

G. CHECK YOUR UNDERSTANDING

Change the following fragments into complete sentences. Add a missing subject or predicate and write the complete sentence on the line below.

Example: Likes music.
Rosa likes music.

1. The great big house.

2. Travel to many different cities.

3. Takes care of children.

4. The fourteen-year-old boy.

5. Looked for food.

H. CHECK YOUR PROGRESS

Rewrite the paragraph below and correct the errors. Look for three irregular past tense verbs errors and two sentence fragments. There is *one* error in each sentence.

> Various native groups in Mexico long ago. The Mayan people builded great pyramids. They haved a form of writing. Were good in art and mathematics. Later they leaved their cities and moved north.

Example: Various native groups *lived* in Mexico long ago.

I. WRITING FOR YOUR PORTFOLIO

In "The Boy Who Took Care of Pigs," Juanito found sticks of silver. Write a story about a person who finds something. The story can be real or imaginary.

Example:

Juanito took care of pigs for a rich man. The pigs looked for food in the woods. The pigs found some special wood. Juanito took the heavy wood home. His father put the wood in their house. Later the government gave them money for the wood. The wood was really silver.

Your Story:

_____

_____

_____

_____

_____

_____

Unit 5

Basanth–The First Day of Spring

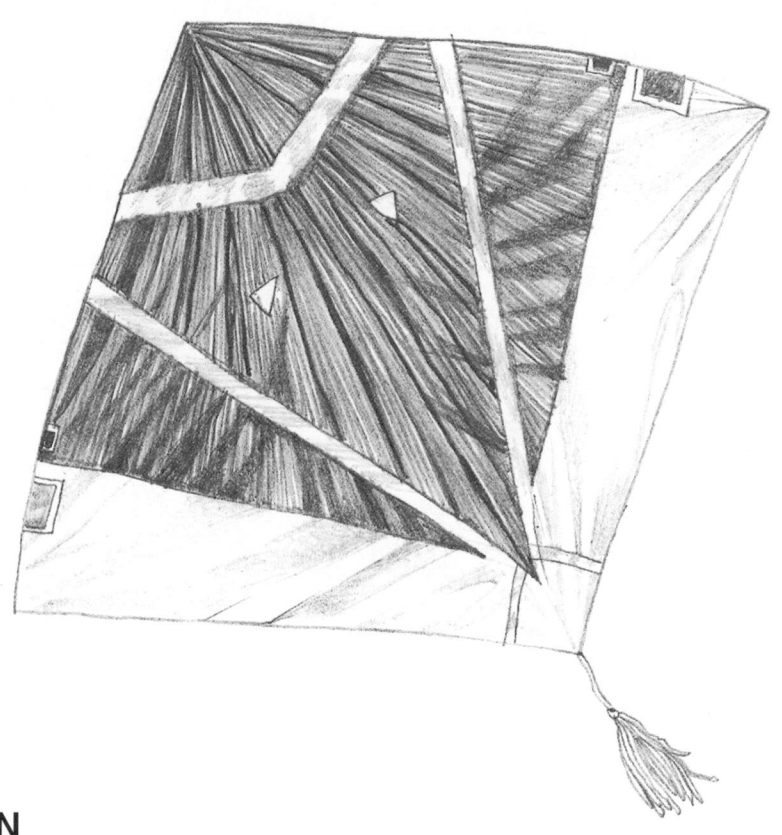

A. INTRODUCTION

1. On which continent is Pakistan? Name two countries that border on Pakistan.

2. Which two of the following statements are true about Pakistan?

    a. Agriculture is important to Pakistan.
    b. About 98% of Pakistanis are Muslims.
    c. Pakistan has the coldest temperatures in all of Asia, including Siberia.

3. How do you celebrate the beginning of spring?

B. READING ACTIVITY

This article is about a Muslim holiday in Pakistan.

1. Reading Selection: Basanth—The First Day of Spring

Alex is a visitor to Pakistan. He is watching Mohammed make a kite for the festival of Basanth.

Alex:	Hey, Mohammed, what are you doing?
Mohammed:	I'm getting ready for Basanth. That's the first day of spring for us.
Alex:	Does everyone celebrate Basanth here in Pakistan?
Mohammed:	Yes, almost everyone celebrates Basanth. Basanth is a Muslim holiday, and almost everyone in Pakistan is Muslim. Other countries also celebrate Basanth, like countries in Africa.
Alex:	What are you making? Is that a kite?
Mohammed:	Yes, I'm making a kite for our kite-flying contest. The contest is part of the festival of Basanth.
Alex:	Why doesn't your kite have a tail?
Mohammed:	This is a Punjabi kite. A Punjabi kite doesn't have a tail. We make the string stiff with starch and water.
Alex:	What are you doing right now?
Mohammed:	I'm putting powdered glass on the string. Then the string has a sharp edge. During the contest, I try to cut the string of the other competitors' kites.
Alex:	When is Basanth?
Mohammed:	It's next week, the end of January. Sometimes, though, Basanth is in the beginning of February.
Alex:	Who watches your contest?
Mohammed:	A lot of people will be there. Basanth is a national holiday, and offices are closed.
Alex:	Don't the kites get stuck in the trees?
Mohammed:	At times. Some people climb on the roofs of buildings. Then they avoid the trees.
Alex:	Well, I'll be watching you next week. I hope you win!

Glossary

Muslim a believer in Islam	**powdered** made into small particles	**stuck** caught

UNIT 5

2. Comprehension Check
Answer the following questions about the reading selection.
- **a.** What is Mohammed making?
- **b.** What is the holiday for the first day of spring in Pakistan called?
- **c.** What does Mohammed put on the string?
- **d.** When is Basanth?
- **e.** Do you like to fly kites? Why or why not?

C. LISTENING ACTIVITY

1. Prelistening
There are many countries in the world where children fly kites. What do kites have in common? How are kites different? What shape of kites do you prefer? Are there kite-flying contests in your city?

2. Listening
Listen to information about the kite-flying contest on Basanth. Complete the sentences with the correct subject. Choose your answers from the list below.

two girls the people	Mohammed Abdul	a tall, thin boy Mohammed's kite	a small boy Alex

- **a.** _____ is flying his Punjabi kite.
- **b.** _____ is dancing in the wind.
- **c.** _____ is flying his kite on top of a building.
- **d.** _____ is trying to cut the string on Mohammed's kite.
- **e.** _____ is watching the contest from the street.
- **f.** _____ are watching the contest from their window.
- **g.** _____ is standing next to Mohammed.
- **h.** _____ are yelling and cheering for the kite competitors.

3. Postlistening
What would you prefer to do during a kite contest? Fly a kite? Watch the contest? Yell and cheer for your friend?

D. GRAMMAR

1. **Grammar Explanation**. Study the information and examples below.
   Use the present continuous tense to describe an action that is happening now.

Present Continuous Tense

SUBJECT	VERB "To be"	(NEGATIVE)	MAIN VERB
I	am	(not)	flying a kite.
He She It	is	(not)	watching the kite.
We They You	are	(not)	making a kite.

Contractions with the subject

SUBJECT + VERB "To be"	NEGATIVE	MAIN VERB
I'm	(not)	flying a kite.
He's She's It's	(not)	watching the kite.
We're They're You're	(not)	making a kite.

Contractions with the verbs

SUBJECT	VERB "To be" NEGATIVE	MAIN VERB
He She It	isn't	watching the kite.
We They You	aren't	making a kite.

Use the present continuous tense with expressions such as "right now," "at the moment," and "at present." Use the simple present tense with expressions such as "all the time," "every day," "sometimes," and "always."

Use the simple preesent tense with non-action verbs such as "be," "like," "feel," "see," "know," "have," "need."

Examples: *Present Continuous*   *Simple Present*
I'm flying a kite right now.   *I fly a kite every day.*
She's watching the contest.   *She always watches the contest.*
He isn't making a kite.   *He often makes kites for the contest.*

2. Grammar Practice

Rewrite each sentence using the correct verb in either the simple present tense or the present continuous tense.

Example: Alex (watches) (is watching) Mohammed.
Alex *is watching* Mohammed.

a. Mohammed (gets) (is getting) ready for Basanth right now.

b. People (celebrate) (are celebrating) Basanth every year.

c. Basanth (is) (is being) a Muslim holiday.

d. At present, Mohammed (makes) (is making) a Punjabi kite.

e. A Punjabi Kite (has) (is having) no tail.

f. At the moment, Mohammed (puts) (is putting) powdered glass on the string.

g. Every year many people (watch) (are watching) the kite contest.

h. Mohammed (likes) (is liking) the kite competition.

E. SPEAKING

Ask a partner the following questions. Then change roles.

1. What is the teacher doing right now?
2. What are you doing right now?
3. What am I doing?
4. What do you think your brother or sister is doing right now?

F. LANGUAGE: Run-on Sentences

1. Language Explanation
Read the information about run-on sentences below.

> **Run-on Sentences**
>
> A run-on sentence is two sentences that run together. There are two subjects and two predicates.
> The two sentences should be separate or they should be connected with a conjunction. There are two ways to correct a run-on sentence:
>
> Write a run-on sentence as two separate sentences.
> Connect the two sentences with conjunctions such as "and," "or," and "but."

Examples:

Run-on Sentence	Mohammed likes Alex he is making a kite for him.
Corrected 1:	*Mohammed likes Alex. He is making a kite for him.*
Corrected 2:	*Mohammed likes Alex, and he is making a kite for him.*
Run-on Sentence	Alex wants to make a kite he doesn't know how.
Corrected 1:	*Alex wants to make a kite. He doesn't know how.*
Corrected 2:	*Alex wants to make a kite, but he doesn't know how.*

2. Language Practice

Rewrite the run-on sentences correctly by either making two separate sentences, or by connecting them with a conjunction.

Example: Basanth is the first day of spring it's a festival.
Basanth is the first day of spring. It's a festival.

a. Basanth is a Muslim holiday everyone celebrates this day.

b. Almost everyone in Pakistan is a Muslim there are a few Hindus.

c. Pakistan celebrates Basanth other countries celebrate Basanth also.

d. Mohammed's kite is colorful his kite doesn't have a tail.

e. He is putting glass on his string he wants to cut the other kite strings.

f. Some kites get stuck in the trees some kites don't get stuck.

g. People are watching the contest they are yelling and cheering.

G. CHECK YOUR UNDERSTANDING

Write three run-on sentences about Pakistan and Basanth. Trade your paper with a partner.

1. _____
2. _____
3. _____

H. CHECK YOUR PROGRESS

Rewrite the paragraph and correct the errors. Look for two present continuous errors, two run-on sentences, and one spelling error. There is *one* error in each sentence.

> Mohammed is flying his kite Alex is watching him. The tall man is wanting to cut Mohammed's kite string. Mohammed is able to move his kitte out of the way. His brother is liking to watch Mohammed. Mohammed flies a kite in the contest every year he wants to win the contest.

Example: *Mohammed is flying his kite. Alex is watching him.*

_____

_____

_____

_____

I. WRITING FOR YOUR PORTFOLIO

Write a paragraph about what happens at your house at 6:00 in the evening. Write the paragraph using the present continuous tense. Follow the example below.

Example: My Home

It is now 6:00 in the evening. I am studying for my classes. My mother and sister are cooking dinner. My little brother is helping to set the table. My father is driving home from work. My dog is barking outside the door. He's hungry and wants to eat, too.

Your Paragraph:

_____

_____

_____

_____

Unit 6

The Gauchos

A. INTRODUCTION

1. On which continent is Argentina? Name two countries that border on Argentina.

2. Which two of the following statements are true about Argentina?

    a. Argentina's main language is Spanish.
    b. Argentina is close to the North Pole.
    c. Argentina has a higher literacy (reading and writing) rate than most of Latin America.

3. Would you like to be a cowboy? Why or why not?

B. READING ACTIVITY

This reading tells of the gauchos, the cowboys of Argentina.

1. Reading Selection: The Gauchos

The gauchos are the cowboys of Argentina. The gaucho tradition started in the 1700s. Some of the people in Argentina went to live on the pampas. These people, called gauchos, wanted to live away from the towns. They caught wild horses. They built homes of mud. For food, they ate mostly beef. They drank a tea called "yerba mate." These people also had a special way of dressing. The men wore baggy pants. Usually they carried long knives. Men and women wore leather boots and ponchos. The gauchos liked to play the guitar and sing songs. They lived a simple life.

In the 1800s, the gauchos sometimes worked for the ranchers. The gauchos were good with horses and knives. They helped the ranchers with cattle. In the late 1800s, the railroad came. There were more towns. Fences were built. These changes ended the gaucho way of life.

There are still a few gauchos today. They live in the country and ride horses. The gauchos are an important symbol in Argentina. They represent the lone fighter. The gaucho is brave and loyal. He or she is loyal to family and friends. The gaucho wants to be independent. He doesn't always trust his boss.

The gaucho was important in Argentine literature and music. People sang songs about the gaucho way of life. The gaucho dress is sometimes used in the tango, an Argentine dance.

Glossary		
baggy loose	**cattle** cows	**pampas** open grasslands

2. Comprehension Check
Answer the following questions about the reading selection

   a. When did the gaucho tradition start in Argentina?

   b. Where did the gauchos want to live?

   c. Are there still gauchos in Argentina today?

C. LISTENING ACTIVITY

1. **Prelistening**

    You are going to listen to a story about the tango. Do you know anything about it? Do you know anyone who dances the tango? Where did the tango start?

2. **Listening**

    First read the questions below. Then listen to your teacher read a short story about the tango. Listen for when it started and what it is. After hearing the story, circle the best answer to the questions below.

    a. When did the tango start?

    – In the early 1800s.
    – In the early 1900s.

    b. How are the steps of the tango dancers?

    – The dancers use long steps.
    – The dancers use short, quick steps.

    c. What are the tango songs like?

    – The songs are usually sad stories.
    – The songs are usually happy stories.

    d. What clothes do tango dancers sometimes wear?

    – They sometimes wear the clothes of the gauchos.
    – They sometimes wear the clothes from the 1600s.

    e. Where do people dance the tango?

    – People dance the tango only in Argentina.
    – People dance the tango all over the world.

3. **Postlistening**

    Would you like to see someone dance the tango?

    Why or why not?

    Would you like to learn how to dance the tango?

    Why or why not?

D. GRAMMAR

1. **Grammar Explanation**
   Study the information and examples below.

   > **Nouns: Count and Non-Count**
   >
   > 1. **Count Nouns**
   >   You can count the items in a group of non-count nouns separately, one by one. You can make regular count nouns plural by adding "-s."
   >   **Examples:** *egg - eggs*
   >   *house - houses*
   >   *table - tables*
   >
   >   Use expressions such as "a lot of," "many," or "a few" with count nouns.
   >
   >   **Examples:** There are *many ranches* in Argentina.
   >   There are *a lot of homes*.
   >   There are *a few gauchos* in Argentina today.
   >
   > 2. **Non-count Nouns**
   >   You can't count separate items in a non-count noun. You can't make non-count nouns plural.
   >
   >   **Examples:** *tea, beef, food, mud, sugar, time, independence, importance, loyalty*
   >
   >   Use expressions such as "a lot of," "much," or "a little," with non-count nouns.
   >
   >   **Examples:** They don't drink *much* coffee.
   >   They drink *a lot of* tea.
   >   They use *a little* sugar in their drinks.

2. **Grammar Practice**
   First rewrite each sentence. Choose the expression that completes the sentence correctly. Then, mark the sentences true (**T**) or false (**F**) according to the information from the reading selection.

   Example: There were (many) (much) gauchos in Argentina in the 1700s.
   There were *many* gauchos in Argentina in the 1700s.

	T	F

a. (A few) (a little) gauchos lived in town.

b. The gauchos caught (many) (much) wild horses.

c. The gauchos never ate (many) (much) food.

d. These people ate (many) (much) beef.

e. They liked to sing (many) (much) songs.

f. (A few) (a little) gauchos worked for the railroad.

g. Ranchers in Argentina have (many) (much) cattle.

h. There are still (a few) (a little) gauchos in Argentina today.

E. SPEAKING

Ask a partner the following questions. Then change roles.

1. Do you have many brothers and sisters?
2. Do you read many books?
3. Do you eat a lot of beef? Why or why not?
4. Do you have much independence?
5. Do you have a lot of time to sing or dance?

F. LANGUAGE: Spelling Rules - Plural Nouns

1. **Language Explanation**
   Read the information about the spelling rules for plural nouns below.

   ---

   1. **Regular Nouns**

      a. For most regular nouns we add "-s" to the noun to form the plural.
         Example: cowboy   cowboys
         gaucho   gauchos

      b. For some nouns we add "-es." These nouns end with "ch," "sh," "ss," or "x."
         Example: ranch   ranches
         dress   dresses

      c. For nouns that end with a consonant + "y," we change the "y" to "i" and add "-es."
         Example: country   countries
         city   cities

      d. For nouns that end with "f" or "fe," we change the "f" to "v" and add "-es."
         Example: knife knives   wife wives

   2. **Irregular Nouns**

      We must learn the separate forms for the plural forms of irregular nouns.
      Example: man men   woman women   child children

   ---

2. **Language Practice**
   Write the plural forms of the singular count nouns below.

   a. ranch _____
   b. city _____
   c. church _____
   d. woman _____
   e. box _____
   f. knife _____
   g. baby _____
   h. song _____
   i. plant _____
   j. rancher _____
   k. child _____
   l. wife _____
   m. country _____
   n. dress _____
   o. life _____
   p. man _____
   q. person _____
   r. fly _____
   s. boss _____
   t. wolf _____

G. CHECK YOUR UNDERSTANDING

Write three sentences using all the nouns below. Use the expressions "many," "a few," "one," or "no" in your sentences.

box   knife   baby   brush   wife   boss   home   couch   magazine

Example: *I have many boxes, a few knives, one baby and no brushes.*

1. _____

2. _____

3. _____

H. CHECK YOUR PROGRESS

Rewrite the paragraph below and correct the errors. Look for three errors in the expressions before nouns, three spelling errors, and one sentence fragment. There is *one* error in each sentence.

> There were much gauchos in the 1700s and 1800s. The men lived with their wifes in mud houses. They lived far away from the citys. Rode horses. The childs didn't go to school. The families ate many beef. Much gauchos worked for the ranchers.

Example: There were *many* gauchos in the 1700s and 1800s.

_____

_____

_____

_____

_____

I. WRITING FOR YOUR PORTFOLIO

Write an informative paragraph about a country. Use your own knowledge or research a country. In your paragraph, use expressions such as "many," "much," "a few," and "a little."

Example: Argentina

Argentina has many different regions. There are high mountains, the pampas, forests, and plateaus. The native people were the first inhabitants. Later people from many countries in Europe came to Argentina. Today there is much immigration from other countries in South America to Argentina. Only a few people come from outside South America.

Your Paragraph:

_____

_____

_____

_____

_____

Unit 7

The Mouse Bride

A. INTRODUCTION

1. On which continent is Finland? Name two countries that border on Finland.

2. Which two of the following statements are true about Finland?
    a. Finland is one of the closest countries to the South Pole.
    b. Skiing and skating are popular sports in Finland.
    c. During the winter, temperatures often fall below zero in Finland.

3. How does a man usually find his bride?

B. READING ACTIVITY

This story from Finland is about a young man who was looking for a bride.

1. Reading Selection: The Mouse Bride

Pekka had three sons. One day Pekka told his sons, "It is time for you to get married. Each of you will walk in a different direction. There you will find your wife."

The youngest son was named Jukka. He went into the forest. He was walking in the woods for three days when he saw a tiny house. He knocked, but there was no answer. He went inside. A little gray mouse was sitting on the table.

"Welcome," said the little mouse. "Why are you so sad?" Jukka answered, "I was looking for my bride. But no one is home." "Marry me, and you will never be sorry," said the mouse. "Why not?" he said. "I have no other to marry." Jukka walked home to tell his father. All three brothers had found brides.

Pekka told his sons, "Bring home the brides on Midsummer's Day. Then you will be wed."

Two months later, Jukka returned to the house of the mouse bride. He was worried. What would his father and brothers say about a mouse bride?

The little mouse was waiting for him. She climbed into a tiny carriage. Five mice led the carriage. Jukka walked slowly next to the carriage through the forest. As the carriage was crossing a bridge, a big boy saw them. "What is this?" The boy kicked the mice and carriage into the river. Jukka was going to hit the boy, but the boy ran away.

Jukka looked into the river. Suddenly five gray horses and a lovely carriage rose from the water. Inside the carriage was a beautiful young woman.

"What happened?" asked Jukka.

"Once I was a king's daughter. A witch put a spell on me. The spell could not be broken until a young man asked me to marry him, and another young man tried to kill me. Now the spell is broken." "How wonderful! Let's hurry home," said Jukka.

All three brothers arrived with their brides. They were all married in the their father's house. After everyone sang and danced, Jukka and his bride went home. The small house in the forest was now a castle. Jukka and his mouse bride lived happily ever after.

Glossary		
carriage a vehicle with wheels for carrying people	**Midsummer's Day** the middle of summer	**spell** words having magical power

UNIT 7

   2. Comprehension Check
   Answer the following questions about the reading selection.
   a. What does the father tell his three sons to do?
   b. What does Jukka, the youngest son, find?
   c. How was the magic spell on the mouse bride broken?

C. LISTENING ACTIVITY

   1. Prelistening
   Do you know any stories about princesses? How are they similar to this story? How are they different?

   2. Listening
   Read the story again. Then listen to the following questions about the story. Write the answers to the questions in the spaces provided.

   a. _____   f. _____

   b. _____   g. _____

   c. _____   h. _____

   d. _____   i. _____

   e. _____   j. _____

   3. Postlistening
   Which story do you like better—the story you know about a princess, or the story from Finland about a mouse bride?

D. GRAMMAR

   1. Grammar Explanation
   Study the information and examples below.

   > **Past Continuous Tense**
   >
   > Use the simple past to describe a completed action in the past.
   > **Example:** *He saw a tiny house.*
   >
   > Use the past continuous tense to describe an ongoing action in the past. You form the past continuous tense by using the past tense of the verb "to be" (was/were) and adding "-ing" to the main verb.
   > **Examples:** *Jukka was walking in the forest.*
   > *The brothers were looking for brides.*

2. Grammar Practice

First change the verb in parentheses to the past continuous tense. Then, mark the sentences true (**T**) or false (**F**) according to the information from the reading selection.

Example: Pekka _____ (talk) but the sons didn't listen.
Pekka *was talking* but his sons didn't listen.   (F)

a. All three sons _____ (walk) in the same direction to find a bride.   (   )

b. Jukka _____ (walk) in the forest for ten days before he found a house.   (   )

c. In the house, a little mouse _____ (dance) on the table.   (   )

d. Jukka told the mouse he _____ (look) for a bride.   (   )

e. When Jukka later returned, two cats _____ (wait) for him.   (   )

f. As the carriage _____ (cross) a bridge, a big boy saw them.   (   )

g. Jukka _____ (kick) the carriage as the boy tried to stop him.   (   )

h. Jukka _____ (go) to hit the boy, but the boy ran away.   (   )

i. The carriage and horse (rise) from the water. _____   (   )

j. After the three weddings, everyone _____ (sing).   (   )

E. SPEAKING

Ask a partner the following questions. Then change roles.

1. What were you doing at 3:00 PM yesterday?
2. What were you doing at 6:00 PM yesterday?
3. What were you doing at 9:00 PM yesterday?
4. What were you doing at 7:00 AM this morning?
5. What were you doing at 9:00 AM this morning?

F. LANGUAGE

1. Language Explanation
Read the information about prepositions of time below.

Prepositions of Time

1. **at**
   Use "at" with time of day.
   Examples: at 3:00   at noon   at midnight   at 11:30

2. **on**
   Use "on" with dates and days.
   Examples: on June 21st   on Midsummer's Day   on Thursday

3. **in**
   Use "in" for longer periods of time, such as months, years, and seasons. Also use "in" for morning, afternoon, evening.
   Examples: in June   in 1970   in the summer
                  in the morning in the afternoon in the evening

---

2. Language Practice
Write the correct preposition for each expression. Use "at," "on," or "in."

Example: _____ midnight
            __at__ midnight

a. 12:15 _____

b. 1986 _____

c. summer _____

d. July _____

e. midnight _____

f. Christmas Day _____

g. the morning _____

h. September _____

i. Monday _____

j. noon _____

k. New Year's Day _____

l. 1991 _____

m. the evening _____

n. 9:05 _____

o. winter _____

p. May 12th _____

G. CHECK YOUR UNDERSTANDING
Complete the blanks in the following story. Use the prepositions "at," "on," or "in."

Jukka met the mouse bride _____ April. He first saw her _____ the morning. He left the house _____ the afternoon. Two months later, he returned to the mouse bride. They left her tiny house _____ Thursday and arrived at Jukka's home _____ Saturday. Jukka and his bride married _____ Midsummer's Day _____ 3:00 _____ the afternoon.

H. CHECK YOUR PROGRESS
Rewrite the paragraph and correct the errors. Look for two errors in past continuous, three errors in prepositions, and one spelling error. There is *one* error in each sentence.

> Olga was live happily in her father's castle. A witch came on the winter to the castle. Olga was sing when the witch saw the princess. The wich put a spell on Olga and Olga became a mouse. Five years later at April, Jukka met the mouse. Jukka broke Olga's spell in June 20th.

Example: Olga *was living* happily in her father's castle.

_____

_____

_____

_____

UNIT 7

I. WRITING FOR YOUR PORTFOLIO

Write an autobiographical paragraph about (yourself). Write about what you were doing two years ago. Use the past continuous tense.

Example: Two Years Ago

Two years ago, I was living in Guadalajara. I was staying with a Mexican family for two months. I was going to school to learn Spanish. On the weekends I was traveling around the city. I was having lots of fun.

Your Paragraph:

_____

_____

_____

_____

_____

Unit 8

The Lion and the Hare

A. INTRODUCTION

1. On which continent is Iran? Look at a map and name two countries that border on Iran.

2. Which two of the following statements do you think are true about Iran?

    a. The major religion in Iran is Islam.
    b. Almost all of the country of Iran is forest land.
    c. Iran is a country in the area called the Middle East.

3. Do you know a famous story about the turtle and the hare? What happens in that story?

UNIT 8

B. READING ACTIVITY

This is a Persian tale about a hare trying to trick a lion. The country now known as Iran was formerly called Persia.

1. Reading Selection: The Lion and the Hare

Long ago the wild animals lived well together in a beautiful land. Then a cruel lion came to live in their area. He attacked the animals. The animals decided on a plan. They told the lion, "We live in fear because you attack us. Promise not to attack us anymore. Then we will send you one animal a day for your meals." The lion agreed.

One day the hare was to be the lion's dinner. The hare didn't want to be eaten. He told the other animals, "I have a plan. I myself can rescue you from this terrible thief. Give me some extra time." The animals agreed. Several hours passed. The lion was angry. Where was his dinner? The hare ran into the lion's home. He was out of breath.

"I didn't receive my dinner!" shouted the lion angrily. "I was bringing you a rabbit, but another lion took it for himself. I told him the dinner was for our chief. The other lion didn't care. He said he was the new chief," said the hare.

The lion shouted, "Take me to this lion! I want to see him for myself!" The hare took the lion to a well. The water in the well was like a mirror. The hare looked in the well. He saw himself reflected. The hare said, "I can't see the lion. Hold me up. Then I can see better." The lion held the hare, then looked in the well. He saw a reflection of himself holding the rabbit. He was very angry. He thought he saw another lion holding his rabbit.

The lion roared. He put down the hare, then jumped into the well. The lion drowned in the water of the well.

All the animals were relieved to hear of the lion's death. They gave themselves a big party.

Glossary	
hare a larger species of rabbits	**relieved** to be freed of fear or pain
drowned died in the water	**well** a hole drilled in the earth to get water

2. Comprehension Check
Answer the following questions about the reading selection.

a. What was the agreement the animals made with the lion?

b. Why did the hare make a plan to kill the lion?

c. Why did the lion jump in the well?

d. Did the hare save himself using his brain or his muscles?

C. LISTENING ACTIVITY

1. **Prelistening**
   Did you know how this story was going to end? Do you know any other stories about hares? Do you know any other stories about lions? Describe them.

2. **Listening**
   Listen to quotes from the animals in the story. Decide who is talking: the lion, the hare, or the other animals. Circle the correct answer for each quote.

   a. the lion / the hare / the other animals
   b. the lion / the hare / the other animals
   c. the lion / the hare / the other animals
   d. the lion / the hare / the other animals
   e. the lion / the hare / the other animals
   f. the lion / the hare / the other animals

3. **Postlistening**
   What are other times that brains win over muscle? Describe an experience that you had.

D. GRAMMAR: Reflexive Pronouns

1. **Grammar Explanation**
   Study the information and examples below.

   Reflexive Pronouns

   Reflexive pronouns refer to the subject of the sentence. Reflexive pronouns can emphasize a person or a thing in the sentence.

   NOTE: Phrases such as "by myself" or "by himself" mean alone or without help.

Subject Pronouns	Reflexive Pronouns
I →	myself
you →	yourself, yourselves
he →	himself
she →	herself
we →	ourselves
they →	themselves

   Examples: He saw *himself* in the well. (refers to subject)
   They gave *themselves* a party. (refers to subject)
   We *ourselves* solved the problem. (emphasis)
   I killed the lion by *myself*. (alone, without help)

2. Grammar Practice

First change the subject pronoun in parentheses to its corresponding reflexive pronoun. Then, mark the sentences true (**T**) or false (**F**) according to the information from the reading selection.

Example: The lion lived by (him) in a beautiful land.
The lion lived by *himself* in a beautiful land. (**F**)

                                                                                                         T   F

a. The animals could not help (they) against the attack of the lion.

b. The hare said, "I (I) can rescue you from this terrible thief."

c. The animals said, "We want to kill the lion by (we)."

d. The hare told the lion another lion took the rabbit for (he).

e. The lion said to the hare, "You (you) took the other rabbit."

f. The hare could see (he) in the water of the well.

g. The lion and the hare could not see (they) in the water of the well.

h. However, the lion didn't know he was seeing (he) in the water.

i. The hare killed the lion all by (he).

j. Then the animals gave (they) a big party.

E. SPEAKING

Ask a partner the following questions. Then change roles.

1. Do you like to look at yourself in the mirror or in photographs? Why or why not?
2. Do you like to stay home by yourself?
3. Do your parents drive themselves to work?
4. Did you come to school by yourself?
5. What can only you yourself do that is extra special?
6. Do you like to make things by yourself? Give an example.

F. LANGUAGE

1. Language Explanation

Read the information about the spelling rules for using "i" and "e" together below.

> **Spelling Rules: Using "i" and "e" Together**
>
> Here is a short poem to help remember the "i" and "e" spelling rules:
>
> Use "i" before "e,"
> Except after "c,"
> Or when sounding as "a," as in "neighbor" and "weigh."
>
> **Examples:** *chief, believe, piece, relieve, thief* (rule in line 1)
> *receive, ceiling, deceive, receipt* (rule in line 2)
> *eight, weight* (rule in line 3)

2. Language Practice

Complete the blanks in the following words, using the "i" and "e" spelling rules.

a. n _____ ce
b. ch _____ f
c. c _____ ling
d. n _____ ghbor
e. rec _____ pt
f. rel _____ ve
g. th _____ f
h. w _____ gh
i. ach _____ ve
j. f _____ ld

k. bel _____ ve
l. w _____ ght
l. br _____ f
m. dec _____ ve
n. p _____ ce
o. _____ ght
p. rec _____ ve
q. perc _____ ve
r. pr _____ st
s. sh _____ ld

UNIT 8

G. CHECK YOUR UNDERSTANDING
Choose six words from the exercise on the previous page. Write a sentence with each word.

1. _____
2. _____
3. _____
4. _____
5. _____
6. _____

H. CHECK YOUR PROGRESS
Rewrite the paragraph and correct the errors. Look for two reflexive pronoun errors, two spelling errors with "i" and "e" used together, and two comma errors. There is *one* error in each sentence.

> Iran borders on the countries of Iraq Russia and Afghanistan. The country officially calls myself the Islamic Republic of Iran. Long ago the country was called Persia and people called himselves Persians. Most of the people beleive in the religion of Islam. There are different ethnic groups in Iran, including Arabs Kurds and Lurs. The cheif language is Farsi.

Example: *Iran borders on the countries of Iraq, Russia, and Afghanistan.*

_____

_____

_____

_____

UNIT 8

I. WRITING FOR YOUR PORTFOLIO

Write a paragraph about yourself. Include two things you like to do by yourself and two things you don't like to do by yourself. Give a reason for each example.

Example: By Myself

There are some things I like to do by myself and some things I don't like to do by myself. I like to go shopping by myself. Then I can go to any store I like. I also like to sleep in a room by myself. That's because my brother talks in his sleep. I don't like to go to movies by myself. I think it's fun to talk to someone about the movie later. Another thing I don't like to do by myself is to travel. I like to see places with other people.

Your Paragraph:

_____

_____

_____

_____

_____

_____

Unit 9

Manatees

A. INTRODUCTION

1. Which continent is Cuba near? Find two countries that are close to Cuba.

2. Which two in the following are true about Cuba?
    a. Sugar is Cuba's most important crop.
    b. Cuba has a warm climate.
    c. The official language of Cuba is Swedish.

3. What do you already know about manatees?

B READING ACTIVITY

This reading describes a mammal that lives in the rivers and along the coast of Cuba.

1. **Reading Selection:** Manatees

   There are many different species of mammals in Cuba. One of the more unusual of these mammals is the manatee. Another name for this animal is the sea cow. Manatees like to live near the coastal waters or rivers in the tropical areas of the world.

   Manatees are gray to black in color. They have front legs like flippers and no legs in back. Their tails are powerful. Manatees can grow to about 15 feet and weigh up to 1,922 pounds. They have a heavy skeleton. A similar species to the manatee is the whale. The manatee is smaller and less powerful than a whale, however.

   The manatee likes to be with other manatees. They play together, hug each other with flippers, and even press lips together like a kiss. They eat 60-100 pounds of food per day.

   They like to eat grasses and different plants that grow in the water. They use their flippers to clean their teeth and rub their sides. Manatees can go under water for up to 16 minutes at a time.

   Female manatees have one offspring every two to five years. Occasionally they have twins. The offspring is born under water. The mother brings the young up to the air on her back.

   These animals are slow and not very careful. Sometimes they are hurt by boats. These animals are now an endangered species. They were almost extinct about 40 years ago.

Glossary			
endangered species things in danger of extinction, or dying out	**flipper** a limb, similar to an arm, used for swimming	**offspring** the young of a person or animal	**species** a group of living things that are similar

2. **Comprehension Check**
   Answer the following questions about the reading selection.

   a. Where does the manatee like to live?

   b. How do manatees play with other manatees?

   c. What do manatees eat?

   d. What is a problem with manatees and their future?

UNIT 9

C. LISTENING ACTIVITY

1. Prelistening
Look at the illustrations below of a seal, a walrus, and a whale. What are some comparisons you can make about these animals as compared to the manatee? Which seems larger? More powerful? Longer? Slower?

2. Listening
First listen to the following comparisons between manatees and other mammals. Then mark the sentences true (**T**) or false (**F**), according to the information you hear.

a. Manatees are heavier than seals. ( )
b. Manatees are larger than whales. ( )
c. Manatees are less powerful than whales. ( )
d. Manatees are bigger than seals. ( )
e. Manatees are longer than walruses. ( )
f. Manatees are slower than seals. ( )
g. Manatees have offspring more often than seals do. ( )
h. Manatees are more endangered than walruses. ( )

Walrus

Antarctic Fur Seal

3. Postlistening
Were you correct in your guesses in comparing the seal, walrus, whale, and manatee?

What information about these animals was surprising to you?

Whale

D. GRAMMAR

1. Grammar Explanation
Study the information and examples below.

> **Comparative Form of Adjectives**
>
> Use the comparative form of an adjective to compare two objects or people. Use "than" before the second object or person compared. The rules for forming the comparative adjective change according to the number of syllables and the spelling of the adjective.
>
> **One Syllable**
> large → larger
> big → bigger
>
> **Two-syllables ending in -y**
> heavy → heavier
> happy → happier
>
> **Two or more syllables**
> endangered → more endangered
> powerful → more powerful
>
> **Other forms:**
> good → better   bad → worse   little → less
>
> **Examples:** Manatees are heavier than seals.
> Whales are larger than manatees.
> Manatees are less powerful than whales.

2. Grammar Practice

Look at the chart below about the manatee and the walrus. Answer the questions using the comparative form of the adjective in parentheses.

Average statistics	Manatee	Walrus
Length	15 feet	11 feet 10 inches
Weight	1,922	2,783 pounds
Hairiness	a little hair	almost no hair
Length of time under water	16 minutes	30 minutes
Amount of food consumed daily	60-100 pounds a day	100 pounds daily

Example: Which mammal is (long)?
The manatee is longer than the walrus.

a. Which mammal, the manatee or the walrus, is (heavy)?

_____

b. Which mammal is (small) overall?

_____

c. Which mammal stays under water for a (long) time?

_____

d. Which mammal eats (large) amounts of food?

_____

e. Which animal is (hairy)?

_____

E. SPEAKING

Ask a partner the following questions. Then change roles.

1. Which is the tallest animal you know?
2. Which is bigger, Cuba or the United States?
3. Which is warmer, the ocean water around Cuba or around Alaska?
4. Which can run faster, a cat or a dog?
5. Which is larger, a seal or a manatee?

F. LANGUAGE

1. **Language Explanation**
   Read the information about punctuation rules for using the colon below.

   ### Punctuation Rules: The Colon

   1. Use a colon to introduce a series or list. Do not use colons with a series or a list that comes after a verb or a preposition.

      Examples: *Other kinds of sea mammals are as follows: whales, seals, and walruses.*
      Manatees live in these areas: North America, Brazil, and Africa.
      (Incorrect) Other kinds of sea mammals are: whales, seals, and walruses.

   2. Use a colon to follow the salutation in a formal or business letter.

      Examples: *Dear Ms. Ramos: Dear Manager: Dear Buyer:*

2. **Language Practice**
   Rewrite the sentences below. Use a colon when needed. Put a check mark next to sentences where colons are not needed.

   Example: Manatees live in these areas North America, Brazil, and Africa.
   Manatees live in these areas: North America, Brazil, and Africa.

   a. Other kinds of sea mammals are as follows whales, seals, and walruses.
   _____

   b. Other kinds of sea mammals are whales, seals, and walruses.
   _____

   c. There are other kinds of mammals in Cuba rodents, sloths, and bats.
   _____

   d. Other kinds of mammals in Cuba are rodents, sloths, and bats.
   _____

   e. Examples of birds in Cuba include buzzards, parrots, and flamingoes.
   _____

   f. Examples of birds in Cuba are as follows buzzards, parrots, and flamingoes.
   _____

   g. In Cuba, some of the reptiles are crocodiles, tortoises, and iguanas.
   _____

   h. Here is a list of different reptiles in Cuba crocodiles, tortoises, and iguanas.
   _____

G. CHECK YOUR UNDERSTANDING

Make a list of five of your favorite animals. Use a colon correctly in your list.

Example: I like these animals: giraffes, manatees, lions, whales, and parrots.

H. CHECK YOUR PROGRESS

Rewrite the paragraph and correct the errors. Look for three errors with comparative adjectives, two colon errors, and one sentence fragment. There is *one* error in each sentence.

> Two other mammals in Cuba are: bats and sloths. Sloths are heavy than bats. In Cuba, you can find the following bats butterfly bat, fisherman bat, and evening bat. The fisherman bat is large than the butterfly bat. The butterfly bat the smallest of all bats in the world.

Example: *Two other mammals in Cuba are bats and sloths.*

UNIT 9

I. WRITING FOR YOUR PORTFOLIO

Write a formal letter to request information on an animal you like. Ask questions about the animal. Include your address, the date, the salutation, the request, a closing, and your name and signature.

Example:

4364 Elm St.
Los Angeles, CA 90041

November 18, 2002

To Whom It May Concern:

I would like to receive information about the manatee. I think the manatee is a very fascinating animal. I want to know more about where manatees live. I'd also like to know the following about the manatee: eating habits, life span, weight, and enemies.

Thank you for your help.
Regards,

Alex Bradley
Alex Bradley

Your Letter:

_____

_____

_____

_____

_____

Unit 10

Three Major Cities

A. INTRODUCTION

1. On which continent is the United States? What two countries border on the United States?

2. Which two of the following statements are true about the United States?
   a. All of the people in this country are of the same race.
   b. This country is one of the largest in population in the world.
   c. There are 50 states in this country.

3. What are some places you usually find in a large city?

UNIT 10

B. READING ACTIVITY

This reading describes New York City, Chicago, and Los Angeles—the three largest cities in the United States.

1. Reading Selection: Three Major Cities

New York City is the largest city in the United States. This city is very important to the nation's business and culture. Its people live in a small land area. There are wonderful things to see and do in New York. Some of the tallest buildings in the world were in New York City. Three famous ones were the Twin Towers and the Empire State Building. Terrorists destroyed the Twin Towers on September 11, 2001. There are many theaters and art museums in the city. The Statue of Liberty is in the harbor. Many immigrants coming to New York pass by this statue. About one of four people in New York City was born outside of the United States.

The city of Los Angeles is located between the Pacific Ocean and the San Gabriel Mountains. It is the second largest city in the United States. Los Angeles started as a Mexican town in 1781. It grew quickly in the 20th century. Cars are the most popular way of transportation in the area. As a result, many traffic problems occur. Smog is also a problem. The combination of sun and smoke from cars and industries causes smog. The population of the city is diverse. The largest ethnic group is the Latinos. Immigrants from Asian countries also live in the area. Asian groups include Japanese, Chinese, Koreans, Filipinos, Vietnamese, Thais, and Indonesians. People enjoy outdoor activities. Los Angeles is a center for industry, banking, and entertainment. The city makes most of the nation's movies. There are also many major television studios in the Los Angeles area.

Chicago is in the state of Illinois. It is the third largest city in the United States. It has the third tallest building in the world, the Sears Tower. This city is also known for dramatic changes in weather. January's average temperature is 26.8º F. The average temperature in July is 74.8º. The wind affects the weather also. Chicago has a diverse population. African-Americans and Latinos are the major ethnic groups there. This city is also a center of transportation for railroads, airlines, and roads. Many colleges and universities are in Chicago. Professional sports are big in Chicago. The city has professional teams for baseball, football, hockey, basketball, and soccer.

Glossary	
diverse	different, varied
ethnic	relating to a group of people sharing the same race or nationality, with a common culture
immigrant	a person who comes into another country to live

2. Comprehension Check

Answer the following questions about the reading selection.
1. What are New York City, Los Angeles, and Chicago each known for?
2. What happened in New York on September 11, 2001?
3. Which city is the largest?
4. Which city would you like to visit? Why?

C. LISTENING ACTIVITY

1. **Prelistening**
   Which city in the world do you think is most entertaining? Why? What kinds of activities are there to do in that city?

   a. Los Angeles has the most entertaining places. ☐
      New York City has the most entertaining places. ☐
   b. Los Angeles has the most interesting museums. ☐
      New York City has the most interesting museums. ☐
   c. Los Angeles has the most famous baseball team. ☐
      New York City has the most famous baseball team. ☐
   d. Los Angeles has the most relaxing weather. ☐
      New York City has the most relaxing weather. ☐
   e. Los Angeles has the most wonderful places to visit. ☐
      New York City has the most wonderful places to visit ☐

3. **Postlistening**
   You listened to information about New York City and Los Angeles. Which seems most interesting to you to visit? Why?

D. GRAMMAR

1. **Grammar Explanation**
   Study the information and examples on the following page.

   Use the superlative form of an adjective to compare three or more objects or people. Use "the" before the superlative adjective. The rules for forming the superlative adjective change according to the number of syllables and the spelling of the adjective.

Superlative Form of Adjectives		
One Syllable	**Two-syllables ending in -y**	**Two or more syllables**
large → the largest	pretty → the prettiest	diverse → the most diverse
big → the biggest	happy → the happiest	important → the most important
Other forms:		
good → the best	bad → the worst	little → the least

UNIT 10

Examples: *New York City is the largest in the United States.*
Which city is the prettiest?
Cars are the most popular transportation.

2. Grammar Practice

Look at the chart below with facts about the three cities. Answer the questions using the superlative form of the adjective in parentheses.

	Chicago	Los Angeles	New York City
Buildings	Sear's Tower 1,454' tall	1st Interstate and World Center 1,017'	Empire State Building 1,250'
Bridges	CM & NRR 474' long	Vincent Thomas 1,500'	Verrazano-Narrows 4,260'
Population in 1994	2,731,743 people	3,448,613	7,333,253
Originated	1770s	1781	1626

Example: Which city has the (short) building?
Los Angeles has *the shortest* building.

a. Which city has the (tall) building?

b. Which city has the (long) bridge?

c. Which city is the (populated) city?

d. Which city has the (few) people?

e. Which city has the (small) population?

f. Which is the (old) city?

g. Which is the (young) city?

More Practice

Write the superlative form of the following adjectives:

Example: old   *the oldest*

a. important _____   f. dirty _____

b. easy _____   g. famous _____

c. wonderful _____   h. cold _____

d. popular _____   i. diverse _____

e. windy _____   j. bad _____

E. SPEAKING

Talk to a partner about places in your city or your school. Use the superlative forms of adjectives to describe the places. Some superlative forms of adjectives you could use are "the best," "the most important," "the largest," "the most famous," "the oldest," and "the prettiest."

Example: *The biggest room in our school is the gym.*

F. LANGUAGE

1. **Language explanation**
   Read the information about rules for doubling final consonants below.

   > **Spelling Rule: Doubling Final Consonants**
   >
   > When adding a suffix, double the final consonant of a word if:
   >
   > a. The word has only one syllable and the word ends with one vowel + one consonant
   >
   > **Examples:**   big + est = biggest   sit + ing = sitting   drop + ed = dropped
   >
   > b. The accent for the word falls on the last syllable and the last syllable has one vowel + one consonant
   >
   > **Examples:**   occur + ed = occurred   control + ing = controlling

UNIT 10

2. Language Practice

Add the suffixes to the words below. Follow the spelling rules for doubling final consonants.

a. hot + est _____

b. stop + ed _____

c. cold + est _____

d. occur + ing _____

e. drop + ing _____

f. refer + ing _____

g. big + est _____

h. short + est _____

i. long + est _____

j. swim + er _____

G. CHECK YOUR UNDERSTANDING

Write a paragraph using four of the words from the exercise above.

_____

_____

_____

_____

_____

H. CHECK YOUR PROGRESS

Rewrite the paragraph and correct the errors. Look for three superlative form errors, two spelling errors, and one apostrophe error. There is *one* error in each sentence.

> The famousest fire in Chicago was over one hundred years ago. It occured in 1871. Some say Patrick O'Learys cow started it. It was bigest fire in Chicago history. One third of the city was desstroyed. Many of the most large buildings were burned.

_____

_____

_____

_____

UNIT 10

I. WRITING FOR YOUR PORTFOLIO

Write a paragraph comparing three places you know. Use superlative adjectives.

Example: Three Cities

Chicago, Los Angeles, and New York City are the three largest cities in the United States. Some of the tallest buildings in the world were in New York City. In Los Angeles, cars are the most popular form of transportation. Chicago has the third tallest building in the world. Many people live in these three cities.

Your Paragraph:

_____

_____

_____

_____

_____

Unit 11

The Sahara Desert

A. INTRODUCTION

1. On which continent is Algeria? Name two countries that border on Algeria.

2. Which two of the following statements are true about Algeria?
   a. Algeria is the smallest country in Africa.
   b. Algeria borders on the ocean.
   c. Part of the Sahara Desert is found in Algeria.

3. What do you already know about the Sahara Desert?

B. READING ACTIVITY

The Sahara Desert crosses many countries in Africa, including Algeria.

1. Reading Selection: The Sahara Desert

The Sahara Desert is the largest desert in the world. It goes across the northern part of Africa, crossing many countries. Algeria is one of these countries. Almost 80% of Algeria is desert. There are mountains on the northern edge of the Algerian Sahara. There are also rock formations in the southeastern part of the desert. One huge rock is Mount Tahan. Mount Tahan sometimes has snow on top. The desert is very hot. At times the temperature in the desert is 110º F. When the sun goes down, it is cold at night. There are also days of wind and blowing sand. The desert has hills of sand, called sand dunes. These sand dunes move in the wind.

Oil Rig

Less than 3% of the Algerians live in the desert. Most desert people live in oasis towns. You can usually find water and often palm trees there. People build houses, mosques, and a market place at the oasis. A few nomads travel across the desert in Algeria. They live in tents made of goats' hair, wool, and grass. The nomads travel between pastures with their camels and other animals. In the northeast, there are rigs to take out the oil and natural gas in the desert. Trucks are the main means of transportation across the desert. They travel on roads across the desert. Sand on the road is always a problem. There are still a few camel caravans that cross the desert.

There is little natural life in the desert. There are some snakes, sand rats, lizards, and desert foxes. There are also a few plants. During the heat of the day, most animals stay underground. They hunt for food at night.

Glossary

caravan a group of travelers or nomads traveling together
nomads traveling people with no permanent homes
oasis a green area in a desert

2. Comprehension Check
Answer the following questions about the reading selection.
a. How big is the Sahara Desert?
b. What is the desert like? Describe it.
c. Is there life in the desert? Explain.
d. Why is it difficult to live in the desert?

UNIT 11

C. LISTENING ACTIVITY

1. Prelistening
Would you like to live in the desert? Why or why not? Are there deserts in the United States? Describe how you would survive in the desert.

2. Listening
Listen to information about Algeria and the Sahara Desert. Complete the blanks in the paragraph below with the information you hear. Choose from the words in the box to complete the paragraph.

religion	nationality	second	seventh	cross	cities
speak	one	west	north	roads	desert

Algeria is on the _____ coast of Africa. It is the _____ largest country in
                   a   b

Africa. Part of Algeria is covered with the Sahara _____. This desert area has less
                                                        c

than _____ inch of rain a year. Roads now _____ the desert. Sometimes sand
      d   e

covers the _____. Most Algerians live in the farm lands and _____ in the north.
              f   g

The people mostly _____ Arabic. The Muslim _____ is the official religion.
                     h   i

3. Postlistening
What information did you learn about Algeria that you didn't know before?

D. GRAMMAR EXERCISE

1. **Grammar Explanation**
   Study the information and examples below.

   Indefinite Pronouns
   Indefinite pronouns represent people or things in general. Singular indefinite pronouns take singular verbs; plural indefinite pronouns take plural verbs.

Singular				Plural
anybody	anyone	each	either	both
everybody	everyone	nobody	no one	few
none	nothing	one	someone	many
neither				several

   Examples: *Everyone knows about the Sahara Desert.*
   Few live in the Sahara Desert.

2. **Grammar Practice**
   First correct the verb form for each of the following sentences. Then mark the sentences true (**T**) or false (**F**), according to the information you read and heard.

   Example: One of the rocks (is) (are) Mount Tahan.
   One of the rocks *is* Mount Tahan. (**T**)

   a. Several of the deserts in the world (is) (are) larger than the Sahara Desert. ( )

   b. One of the countries within the Sahara Desert (is) (are) Algeria. ( )

   c. Nobody (lives) (live) in the Sahara Desert. ( )

   d. None of the peaks in Algeria (has) (have) snow. ( )

   e. Several of the days in the desert (is) (are) windy. ( )

   f. Many of the desert people (lives) (live) in oasis towns. ( )

   g. Everyone (travels) (travel) in cars to cross the desert. ( )

   h. No one (travels) (travel) on camel in the desert in modern times. ( )

   i. Many of the animals in the desert (stays) (stay) underground during the night. ( )

   j. No one ever (sees) (see) life in the desert. ( )

UNIT 11

E. SPEAKING

With a partner, make five predictions about other students in your class. Start each sentence with an indefinite pronoun. Then talk to the other students to check to see if your predictions are correct.

Examples: *Someone has a black dog.*
Nobody sleeps later than 9:00 in the morning.

F. LANGUAGE

1. Language Explanation
Read the information about antonyms below.

Vocabulary: Antonyms

An antonym is opposite in meaning to another word. We usually refer to the two words as an antonym pair.

Examples: *hot—cold*
young—old
right—wrong

---

2. Language Practice
Choose the correct antonym for each word from the list in the box below. The antonyms are taken from the article on the Sahara Desert.

calm	oasis	temporary	homeowner	solution
artificial	smallest	tiny	southern	several

Example: usually – *rarely*

a. largest _____   f. desert _____

b. northern _____   g. nomad _____

c. permanent _____ h. problem _____

d. natural _____   i. few _____

e. huge _____   j. windy _____

78

G. CHECK YOUR UNDERSTANDING

Write half of ten antonym pairs. Trade papers with a partner. Write the second half to your partner's antonym pairs.

1. _____
2. _____
3. _____
4. _____
5. _____

6. _____
7. _____
8. _____
9. _____
10. _____

H. CHECK YOUR PROGRESS

Rewrite the paragraph and correct the errors. Look for three verb errors, one sentence fragment, and two comma errors. There is *one* error in each sentence.

> In rural Algeria, there is large open markets. Called *souks*. Most of the Algerians shops there. Years ago traders, exchanged goods. People traded food clothing and crafts. Now everyone use money.

Example: In rural Algeria there *are* large open markets.

UNIT 11

I. WRITING FOR YOUR PORTFOLIO

First take a survey of students in your classroom. Ask them about the food they like. Then write a paragraph about the survey. Use indefinite pronouns in your paragraph.

Example: Food Survey

I took a food survey of students in my classroom. Everyone in my class likes pizza. Almost everyone likes chocolate. Eighty percent of the students like popcorn. Some of the students like cola drinks. No one likes lima beans.

Your Paragraph:

_____

_____

_____

_____

_____

The Snow Woman

A. INTRODUCTION

1. Which continent is Japan near? Name two countries that are near Japan.

2. Which two of the following statements are true about Japan?

    a. Japan has a variety of climates, with cold winters in the mountains and hot summers in the south.

    b. Education is not important in Japan, and few people can read and write.

    c. Japan exports many products such as cars, televisions, and radios.

3. "The Snow Woman" is a ghost story. What is a ghost story you know? Does the story have a happy ending?

B. READING ACTIVITY

1. Reading Selection: The Snow Woman

A poor young woodcutter lived near a big forest. To get money, he cut wood and sold the wood. One day he and an old woodcutter went to the forest to cut wood. A big snow storm came. The two men slept in an old empty hut. At midnight the young woodcutter awoke. At the door he saw a beautiful woman. Her face and clothes were white. She went and breathed on the old man. The man turned to ice. She came to the young man. She said, "You are young and handsome. I will not breathe on you. But this is a warning. You must never tell anyone about this night. If you do, you will have a terrible end."

The young woodcutter told no one. A year later, a pretty young woman came to the village. She had no family. The woman's name was Yuke, meaning snow. She was beautiful in face, heart, and spirit. The woodcutter and Yuke fell in love. They soon married. They had a family of four children. Everyone was very happy.

One night the woodcutter and Yuke sat by the fire. They were making presents for their children. The man looked at his wife's face in the light. "You remind me of someone," said the woodcutter. "Tell me the story," said his wife.

The woodcutter told her the story of the snow woman. After he finished, his wife stood up. Her face and clothes turned white. "I told you to tell no one! I should kill you. Now I must leave. Be good to the children. But be careful. If you ever hurt them, I'll come for you." She opened the door and walked out into a snow storm.

You can hear the wind call during a storm. Some say it's the voice of the snow woman, calling for her lost children and home.

Glossary

hut a small house or cabin	**remind** to cause to remember	**warning** a notice of danger

2. Comprehension Check

Answer the following questions about the reading selection.

a. Why didn't the woodcutter tell anyone about what happened the night of the storm?
b. Who really was the woodcutter's wife?
c. Why do you think the Snow Woman didn't kill the woodcutter at the end of the story?

C. LISTENING ACTIVITY

1. Prelistening
Is the ghost in the story a bad ghost? Why or why not?

2. Listening
First read the story about the woodcutter again. Then listen to ten questions about the story and write your answers below.

a. _____

b. _____

c. _____

d. _____

e. _____

f. _____

g. _____

h. _____

i. _____

j. _____

3. Postlistening
Would you change the ending to the story of the snow woman? In what way?

UNIT 12

D. GRAMMAR

1. Grammar Explanation
Study the information and examples below.

Modals: "should," "have to," and "must"	
"should"	**"have to" and "must"**
Use "should" to give advice. Use it to say that something is the good or right thing to do.	Use "have to" and "must" to make a warning or express an obligation. Use them when it is necessary to do something or you are obliged to do it.
Examples:	**Examples:**
I should exercise everyday. *They should go to bed early.*	*I have to get up early every day.* *He has to listen to the snow woman.* *They must get a new car.*

2. Grammar Practice
First choose the answer that is correct according to the story. Then rewrite the sentence on the line below.

Example: The woodcutter (must) (must not) cut wood to get money.
The woodcutter *must* cut wood to get money.

a. The young woodcutter and the old man (have to) (don't have to) go to the forest to cut wood.
___

b. The woodcutter and the old man (should) (should not) go inside the hut to get away from the storm.
___

c. The snow woman said to the woodcutter, "You (must) (must not) tell anyone about this night."
___

d. The woodcutter (has to) (doesn't have to) keep quiet about his night in the storm.
___

e. The woodcutter (should) (should not) tell his wife about the night in the forest.
___

f. Because the woodcutter tells the story, Yuke (must) (must not) leave her home.
___

g. Yuke tells her husband, "You (should) (should not) have a terrible end."
___

h. Yuke warns her husband that he (has to) (doesn't have to) be good to their children.
___

84

E. SPEAKING

Ask a partner the following questions. Then change roles.

1. Do you have to get up early during the week?
2. Should you go to the dentist once a year?
3. What is a chore at home you have to do?
4. What do you think everyone should learn?
5. What is something everyone has to do?

F. LANGUAGE

1. Language Explanation
Read the information about nouns, pronouns, and verbs below.

Parts of Speech: Nouns, Pronouns, and Verbs

Parts of speech are the basic building blocks of language. Parts of speech include nouns, pronouns, verbs, adverbs, adjectives, prepositions, interjections, and conjunctions.

a. Nouns refer to a person, place, or thing (object, idea, or event).
   Examples of persons: *boy, woodcutter, David, actress, baby, woman*
   Examples of places: *forest, Japan, hut, home, village, school, river*
   Examples of things: *snow, wood, ice, heart, spirit, love, presents, story, meeting*

b. Pronouns take the place of a noun or nouns.
   Examples: *she, him, yourself, I, it, anybody, each, everyone, some*

c. Verbs are words that express action or a state of being.
   Examples: *is, are, lived, get, went, slept, will tell, must tell, hurt, opened*

---

2. Language Practice
Identify the part of speech for the underlined words in each sentence.

Example: He cut wood and sold the wood.
   he - pronoun;   sold - verb;   wood - noun

a. They slept in an old empty house. _____

b. A pretty young woman came to the village. _____

c. She was beautiful in face, heart, and spirit. _____

d. If you ever hurt them, I'll come for you. _____

e. You can hear the wind during a storm. _____

UNIT 12

G. CHECK YOUR UNDERSTANDING

Write three sentences. Include nouns, pronouns, and verbs in your sentences. Trade papers with a partner. Tell your partner to put a box around the nouns, to circle the verbs, and to put an 'X' through the pronouns.

1. _____
2. _____
3. _____

H. CHECK YOUR PROGRESS

Rewrite the paragraph and correct the errors. Look for two errors with "should," "have to," or "must"; two capitalization errors; and two spelling errors. There is *one* error in each sentence.

> You should to visit Japan someday. If you go, you must to see the capital of Japan. The city of tokyo is quite modern. There are about 27 million peeple in Tokyo. Tokyo has many parks, Museums, and temples. One beutiful building is the Imperial Palace.

Example: You *should* visit Japan someday.

I. WRITING FOR YOUR PORTFOLIO

Write a paragraph giving someone advice. Give advice about how to do well in school. Use "should," "should not," "have to," "don't have to," "must," and "must not" in your paragraph when possible.

Example: Advice about Getting a Job

Do you want to get a job? You can't just sit at home. You must read the newspaper and look at the want ads. You have to make calls about job openings. You should call friends to see if they have any ideas. You have to keep trying.

Your Paragraph :

Unit 13

Pablo Picasso

A. INTRODUCTION

1. On which continent is Spain? Name two countries that border on Spain.

2. Which two of the following statements are true about Spain?
   a. Claude Monet is a painter who was born in Spain.
   b. Tourists bring in a lot of money to Spain.
   c. Bullfighting is an important event in Spain.

3. What do you know about the artist Picasso?

B. READING ACTIVITY

This reading tells of the life of the famous Spanish artist Pablo Picasso.

1. Reading Selection: Pablo Picasso

Pablo Picasso may be the greatest painter of the 20th century. He was born in Spain in 1881. In addition to being a painter, he was also a sculptor, a ceramist, and a graphic artist. He was a leader in many of the different art movements during the 1900s.

Pablo Ruiz y Picasso was born on the coast of Spain. His father was an art teacher. The father knew that Pablo was very talented. Pablo studied art and was excellent at realistic techniques. He had his own studio in Barcelona at age 16. After a visit to Paris, Pablo decided to move there.

Picasso and other artists reacted against the earlier naturalism in art. From 1901 to 1904, Picasso made paintings with many blue colors. This was called his blue period. Later, between 1905 to 1907, he used more red colors. This was called his rose period. In 1907 he created *Les Demoiselles d'Avignon*. This painting started the way to cubism and abstract art. In cubism Picasso shows his interest in primitive African art.

Possibly Picasso's most famous painting is called *Guernica*. Picasso did this painting in reaction to the bombing of the Spanish town of Guernica. His mural was shown at the Spanish pavilion at the World's Fair of 1937. In his mural, Picasso showed the horrors of war. He used the art techniques of expressionism and cubism. He also used only the colors of black, white, and gray.

Picasso always worked very quickly. He also enjoyed changing his style. Picasso continued working into his 90s. He died in France in 1973.

Glossary
cubism a style of modern art that uses cubes and other geometric forms
mural large painting for a wall
talented having gifts or skills

2. Comprehension Check

Answer the following questions about the reading selection.

a. What was Picasso a leader in?
b. What were two of Picasso's earlier periods?
c. *Les Demoiselles d'Avignon* started the way to what kinds of art?
d. Why is the painting *Guernica* famous?

C. LISTENING ACTIVITY

1. Prelistening
Picasso was famous for his abstract art. This kind of art is not realistic. Lines and colors are more important than realistic objects and people. Do you prefer abstract art or realistic art? Why?

2. Listening
First listen to the explanations of the periods and artistic movements listed in the box below. Then match the names of the periods and artistic movements to the explanations. These all relate to Picasso and his work.

rose period	blue period	expressionism	abstract	cubism

a. _____   e. _____   d. _____

c. _____   b. _____

3. Postlistening
Which of the different kinds of art sounds most interesting to you: expressionism, abstract art, or cubism? Why?

D. GRAMMAR

1. Grammar Explanation
Study the information and examples below.

> **Modals: "may," "might," and "could"**
>
> Use "may," "might," and "could" to show it is possible that something will happen.
>
> **Examples:** *It may be a good idea.*
> *Picasso might be the best artist.*
> *You may draw a good painting in the future.*
> *They could paint a mural.*

2. **Grammar Practice**

First add "may," "might," or "could" to each sentence before the verb in parentheses ( ) and rewrite the sentence. Then mark the sentences true (**T**) or false (**F**) according to the story.

Example: Picasso (be) the greatest sculptor of the 20th century.
Picasso *might be* the greatest sculptor of the 20th century. (**F**)

a. Picasso (be) the greatest painter of the 20th century. ( )

b. Picasso (be) the greatest naturalist artist in the 20th century. ( )

c. If a Picasso painting uses blue colors, it (be) from Picasso's blue period. ( )

d. If a Picasso painting uses red colors, it (be) from Picasso's rose period. ( )

e. Some of Picasso's paintings (show) his interest in primitive African art. ( )

f. *Guernica* (be) Picasso's most famous painting. ( )

g. Picasso (paint) another great painting in the future. ( )

E. SPEAKING

Ask a partner the following questions. Then change roles.

1. Do you think you might be a painter someday?
2. Do you think you may see Picasso's paintings in a museum someday?
3. Do you think you could visit Spain or another country in Europe someday? What might you see there?
4. Do you think you might travel to a foreign country sometime? Which one would you like to visit?

UNIT 13

F. LANGUAGE

1. Language Explanation
Read the information about adjectives, prepositions, and conjunctions below.

> **Parts of Speech: Adjectives, Prepositions, and Conjunctions**
>
> Parts of speech are the basic building blocks of language. Parts of speech include nouns, pronouns, verbs, adverbs, adjectives, prepositions, interjections, and conjunctions.
>
> a. Adjectives describe nouns and pronouns. They answer questions such as "What kind?" "How many?" "Which one?" and "How much?"
>
>   **Examples:** *two, pretty, great, different, realistic, early, red*
>
> b. Prepositions show a relationship between a noun or pronoun and the rest of a sentence. They are always followed by a noun or pronoun.
>
>   **Examples:** *about, after, along, around, at, before, below, beside, between, by, during, for, from, in, into, of, off, on, over, to, under, with, without*
>
> c. Conjunctions connect words, phrases, clauses, or sentences.
>
>   **Examples:** *and, but, or, nor*

2. Language Practice
Identify the part of speech for the underlined words in each sentence.

Example: Picasso was a great painter from Spain.
  great - adjective;   from - preposition

a. Picasso was a wonderful painter, but he did not like naturalism. _____

b. He started the way to two kinds of art: cubism and abstract art. _____

c. Picasso had a blue period and a rose period in his art. _____

d. Picasso's famous painting *Guernica* is about the bombing of Guernica. _____

e. This lovely painting started the way to cubism and abstract art. _____

G. CHECK YOUR UNDERSTANDING

Write three sentences. Include adjectives, prepositions, and conjunctions in your sentences. Trade papers with a partner. Tell your partner to put a box around the adjectives, circle the prepositions, and put an 'X' through the conjunctions.

1. _____

2. _____

3. _____

H. CHECK YOUR PROGRESS

Rewrite the paragraph and correct the errors. Look for two errors with "might," "may," or "could"; one sentence fragment; and three spelling errors. There is *one* error in each sentence.

> You like might to visit Spain someday. In Spain, may you want to see some art museums. The Museum of the Prado in Madrid is a grate art museum. Famous paintings there. Other famus Spanish artists include Diego Velasquez, Francisco de Goya, and Salvador Dali. You coud spend days at the museum.

Example: You *might like* to visit Spain someday.

_____
_____
_____
_____
_____

I. WRITING FOR YOUR PORTFOLIO

Write about a place you would like to visit. Describe activities you might do there. Use "might," "may," and "could" in your paragraph.

Example: My vacation

I would like to visit Los Angeles, California. I might see the Los Angeles County Museum. I want to see the famous paintings there. I could see the television studios. I may go to the beach in the afternoon. I like to swim and make castles in the sand.

Your Paragraph:

_____

_____

_____

_____

_____

Unit 14

The Widow and the Fish

A. INTRODUCTION

1. Which continent is Indonesia near? Name two countries that are near Indonesia.

2. Which two of the following statements are true about Indonesia?
   a. Indonesia has more people than China.
   b. Indonesia has more than 13,000 islands.
   c. Corn is the most widely grown crop in Indonesia.

3. Do you think people should be greedy? Explain.

UNIT 14

B. READING ACTIVITY

This reading is an Indonesian story. It tells about a woman and her faith in Allah, the Islamic name for God.

1. Reading Selection: The Widow and the Fish

Once there was a poor old widow. She lived on the island of Java in Indonesia. She worked hard every day, but it was difficult. Her neighbors were greedy and didn't help her. The woman was not very happy.

One day the widow was walking slowly through the forest. She was very hungry. She saw a dry river with puddles of water. In one of the puddles were three fish. She was filled with joy. She planned to eat the fish for dinner. Suddenly one of the big fish said, "Allah, send us rain! Give us rain before we die!"

The fish repeated the saying over and over again. Quietly the widow watched. After a few hours clouds appeared in the sky. Rain fell and the river filled. The fish swam to safety.

The widow thought and thought. "Maybe I can do the same. I will pray to Allah. Instead of rain, I'll ask for money."

That night the widow called out again and again. "Allah, send me money! Send me money before I die!" The old woman prayed loudly for three days. Her neighbor became very angry. He told the woman to stop calling. Finally he filled a bag with rocks and dirt and climbed on her roof at night. He dropped the bag on the woman as she slept.

In the morning she saw the bag. Inside were coins of gold and silver. "Thank you, Allah!" she said joyfully.

The neighbor heard the news. He was even more angry. He decided to try the same plan for himself. He prayed to Allah. Then he told a servant to drop two bags of rocks and dirt on him. The bags hurt the man. In pain, he opened the two bags. Inside were still rocks and dirt. The man cried out in anger.

The widow lived happily for the rest of her life. The neighbor was unhappy in his greed.

Glossary

greedy wanting more and more	**puddle** small pool of water	**widow** woman whose husband has died

2. Comprehension Check

Answer the following questions about the reading selection.

a. What was the widow's problem?

b. What happened to the fish?

c. How did she solve her problem?

d. Why do you think the neighbor didn't get a bag of gold and silver?

UNIT 14

C. LISTENING ACTIVITY

1. Prelistening
On which item do you think the widow will spend the most money after Allah gives her money? Will she spend more on food? A bed? Clothes? Gifts to the poor?

2. Listening
Listen to the percentage the widow spends on food, a bed, clothes, wood, and the poor. Write the percent and the item in the chart below.

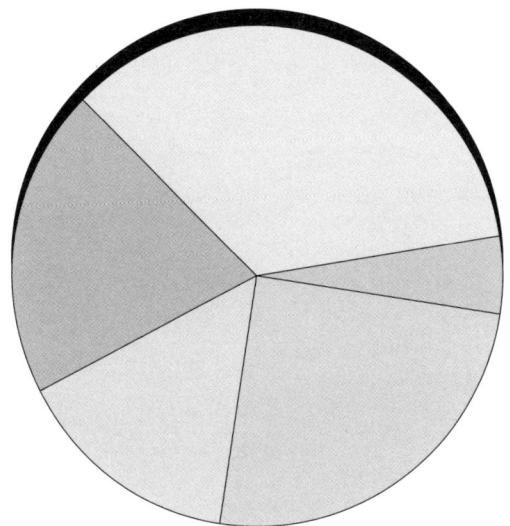

a. _____ % on _____

b. _____ % on _____

c. _____ % on _____

d. _____ % on _____

e. _____ % on _____

3. Postlistening
When you have a good job, do you plan to give money to the poor? Why or why not?

D. GRAMMAR: Adjectives and Adverbs

1. Grammar Explanation
Study the information and examples below.

> **Adjectives and Adverbs**
>
> 1. **Adjectives**
>   Adjectives describe nouns and pronouns. In a sentence, an adjective comes before the noun it is describing. An adjective can also come after the noun or pronoun it is describing if it comes after the verb "to be." Adjectives answer questions such as "What kind?" and "How many?"
>
>   **Examples:** *There was a poor widow.*
>   *She was hungry.*

97

UNIT 14

Adjectives and Adverbs

2. Adverbs

Adverbs modify verbs, adjectives, and other adverbs. In a sentence, an adverb comes near the verb it is modifying or at the beginning or end of the sentence. An adverb can also come before the adjective or other adverb it is modifying. Adverbs answer the questions such as "When?" "Where?" "How?"

Examples: *The neighbor quickly walked home.*
She talked about her vacation slowly.
He was really tired.
She was very intelligent.

3. Spelling Rules

a. Most adverbs are formed with the following rule: adjective + "ly" = adverb

Examples: Adjectives: slow   loud   quick   sudden
Adverb: slowly   loudly   quickly   suddenly

b. Sometimes the adjective ends in "y" and the spelling must change. Here's the rule: Change "y" to "i" and then add the "ly."

Examples: *easy → easily   greedy → greedily   heavy → heavily*

NOTE: A few words are both adjectives and adverbs:
fast   hard   late   early

Examples: *He is late. (adjective)   He went to bed late. (adverb)*
The job is hard. (adjective)   Bill works very hard. (adverb)

2. Grammar Practice

First choose the adjective or adverb to complete the sentence. Then rewrite the sentence.

Examples: There was a (poor) (poorly) widow in the neighborhood.
There was a *poor* widow in the neighborhood.

a. The widow was not very (happy) (happily).

_____

b. The widow worked (hard) (hardly) every day.

_____

c. One day she walked (slow) (slowly) through the forest.

_____

d. (Sudden) (Suddenly) one of the fish spoke.

_____

e. The widow watched the fish (quiet) (quietly).

_____

f. For three days the widow prayed (loud) (loudly).

_____

g. The neighbor (angry) (angrily) dropped a bag on the widow.

_____

h. The widow was (joyful) (joyfully) when she saw the money.

_____

i. The (angry) (angrily) neighbor tried the same plan.

_____

j. The widow was (happy) (happily) for the rest of her life.

_____

E. SPEAKING

Ask a partner the following questions. Then change roles.

1. What is something you do quickly?
2. What is something you do slowly?
3. What is something that makes you angry? What about a friend?
4. What is something that makes you happy?
5. When are you early? When are you late?

F. LANGUAGE

1. **Language Explanation**
   Read the information about antonyms below.

   ### Vocabulary: Antonyms

   An antonym is opposite in meaning to another word. We usually refer to the two words as an antonym pair.

   Examples: *greedy—generous*
   happy—unhappy
   angry—calm
   hungry—satisfied

UNIT 14

2. Language Practice

Choose the correct antonym for each word from the list in the box below.

Example: disbelief _____ *faith*

poor	appear	greedy	walk
joy	loud	faith	hungry
old	quick	angry	happy

a. disbelief _____

b. rich _____

c. calm _____

d. generous _____

e. unhappy _____

f. sorrow _____

g. disappear _____

h. quiet _____

i. satisfied _____

j. run _____

k. slow _____

l. young _____

G. CHECK YOUR UNDERSTANDING

Write ten pairs of antonyms.

Examples: *rich—poor   quick—slow*

1. _____
2. _____
3. _____
4. _____
5. _____
6. _____
7. _____
8. _____
9. _____
10. _____

H. CHECK YOUR PROGRESS

Rewrite the sentences and correct the errors. Look for three adverb/adjective errors, two spelling errors and one run-on sentence. There is *one* error in each sentence.

> The islands of Indonesia are dense populated. People have differently languages and customs in various areas. Most Indonesians follow the religion of Islam they pray daily. The peopel use music and drama in their festivals. Farming is very important to this countrie. The people work hardly for their food.

Example: The islands of Indonesia are *densely* populated.

I. WRITING FOR YOUR PORTFOLIO

Describe an accomplishment of yours. Tell about a time you worked hard to achieve your results. Use five adverbs in your writing.

Example: Summer Job

One summer I worked in the desert. I helped to pick melons. The work was extremely difficult. I picked the melons quickly. I was very hot. One day I nearly fainted from the work. Luckily someone gave me water. I'll never forget that summer.

Your Paragraph:

Unit 15

Helen Keller

A. INTRODUCTION

1. On which continent is the United States? Name two countries that border on the United States.

2. Which two of the following statements are true about the United States?
    a. The United States has a president for a leader of government.
    b. The United States has special education programs for persons with handicaps.
    c. Every state in the United States borders on the ocean.

3. The biography of Helen Keller tells of a handicapped woman who was both blind and deaf. List five problems you would have if you were both deaf and blind.

B. READING ACTIVITY

Helen Keller is a famous American. Here is a biography of her life.

1. Reading Selection: Helen Keller (1880-1968)

Helen Keller was born in Alabama in 1880. At one and a half years old, she had a serious illness. As a result, she became deaf and blind. As Helen grew older, she couldn't communicate. Her family didn't know how to teach her language. They also couldn't control her. At times she hurt her family.

The family learned of a teacher. This teacher, Annie Sullivan, came to live with the family. Helen was six years old at the time. Miss Sullivan was very patient. The teacher spelled letters into Helen's hand. This system is called the manual alphabet. The first word Helen understood was 'water.'

With Annie's help, Helen learned to read and write. She even learned to speak. At age 20, Helen went to college. Annie helped by spelling the lectures to Helen. In 1904, Helen graduated from Radcliffe College with honors.

Helen Keller and her teacher traveled all over the world. Helen spoke about handicapped people. She wanted the handicapped to live like other people. Helen received honors and awards from organizations worldwide. She was one of the founders of the American Foundation of the Blind. She helped to raise millions of dollars for the blind.

During her life, she wrote many books. *The Story of My Life* by Helen Keller was published in 1903.

Glossary		
founder a person who helps to begin an organization	**lecture** a speech given to inform	**manual** using the hands

2. Comprehension Check

Answer the following questions about the reading selection.

a. How did Helen become deaf and blind?
b. At first, why did Helen's family have problems with Helen?
c. How did Annie Sullivan help Helen?
d. What do you admire most about Helen Keller?

UNIT 15

C. LISTENING ACTIVITY

1. Prelistening

Helen Keller had a special teacher in her life. Which special teacher in your life do you remember? Why do you remember that teacher?

2. Listening

First listen to information about Helen Keller. Then, mark the sentences true (**T**) or false (**F**) according to the information you hear.

a. Helen Keller was fourteen months old when she became deaf and blind. ( )

b. Helen's parents took her to see Alexander Graham Bell. ( )

c. Alexander Graham Bell was the famous teacher of the learning handicapped. ( )

d. Alexander Graham Bell was also the inventor of the telephone. ( )

e. Annie Sullivan came to be Helen's teacher. ( )

f. Annie Sullivan stayed with Helen until Annie got married. ( )

g. Helen used only regular textbooks during her college studies. ( )

h. During Helen's life she lectured all over in different places. ( )

i. Helen wrote only one book about her life. ( )

3. Postlistening

Helen Keller accomplished much during her life. Which accomplishment do you find most amazing?

D. GRAMMAR

1. Grammar Explanation
Study the information and examples below.

Indirect Objects

An indirect object comes between the verb and the direct object. The indirect object is always a noun or a pronoun. It can tell *to whom* the action of the verb is done. Or it can tell *to what* the action of the verb is done.

SUBJECT	VERB	INDIRECT OBJECT	DIRECT OBJECT
Anne	taught	Helen	the manual alphabet.
Helen	sent	the foundation	money.
Helen	gave	them	the information.

2. Grammar Practice

First choose the indirect object that makes the sentence true according to the information you know. Then rewrite the sentence.

Example: Helen Keller was deaf and blind.
Helen's family couldn't teach (Annie) (Helen) anything.
Helen Keller was deaf and blind.
Helen's family couldn't teach *Helen* anything.

a. Annie Sullivan was Helen's teacher. She taught (Helen) (Annie) the manual alphabet.

b. The teacher showed (Annie) (Helen) a new world.

c. Helen spoke to thousands of people around the world. She told (them) (it) her life story.

d. Helen gave (the people) (the story) information about the handicapped.

e. Organizations gave (the people) (Helen) many awards.

f. Miss Keller was one of the founders of the American Foundation of the Blind. She gave (herself) (the foundation) millions of dollars.

g. Helen never forgot her teacher Annie Sullivan. She always gave (her teacher) (her sister) credit for her success.

E. SPEAKING

Ask a partner the following questions. Then change roles. Use indirect objects.

1. What present did you give someone in your family?
2. What did you give to a friend?
3. What did you tell your friend today?
4. What did you tell your family yesterday?

F. LANGUAGE

1. Language Explanation

Read the information about suffixes below.

> **Suffixes - "-ful" and "-less"**
>
> A suffix added to the end of a word changes the word's meaning.
> 1. The suffix "-ful" means "full of."
>   **Examples:** *joyful*— full of joy
>   *hopeful*— full of hope
>
> 2. The suffix "less" means "without."
>   **Examples:** *thoughtless*— without thought
>   *thankless*— without thanks

2. Language Practice

First choose the word with the suffix that makes the sentence true. Then rewrite the sentence.

Example: At one and a half years old, Helen Keller was very ill. She became deaf and blind. It was a (joyful) (joyless) time for the family. It was a *joyless* time for the family.

a. The family couldn't teach language to Helen. They felt the situation was (hopeful) (hopeless).

b. The family also couldn't control Helen. At times the girl physically hurt people. Her actions were (hurtful) (hurtless).

c. Then Annie Sullivan came to teach Helen. Annie was (hopeful) (hopeless) about Helen.

d. Annie taught the girl to communicate. The family was very (thankful) (thankless).

e. The first word Helen learned was "water." It was a (joyful) (joyless) moment for everyone.

f. Helen spoke to people around the world. She raised money for the blind. Her actions were (helpful) (helpless).

g. Helen taught people about the handicapped. Sometimes people are (thoughtful) (thoughtless) and say bad things to handicapped people.

h. Helen helped the world in many ways. She was a (wonderful) (wonderless) person.

G. CHECK YOUR UNDERSTANDING

Write about yourself. Write five sentences about times that you were joyful, joyless, hopeful, hopeless, thoughtful, or thoughtless.

Examples: I was *joyful* when my brother was born.
I felt *hopeless* about my grade in science.

1. _____
2. _____
3. _____
4. _____
5. _____

H. CHECK YOUR PROGRESS

Rewrite the paragraph and correct the errors. Look for two verb errors and three spelling errors. There is *one* error in each sentence.

> When Helen Keller was six years old, her parents felt hopeles. They taked Helen to see Alexander Graham Bell. He were a famous teacher of the deaf and the inventor of the telephone. Because of Bell, Annie Sullivan taught Helen how to read and rite. Annie was very helpfull.

Example: When Helen Keller was six years old, her parents felt hopeless.

UNIT 15

I. WRITING FOR YOUR PORTFOLIO

Write a paragraph about a challenge you faced. Think of something difficult that you faced in your life. Write how you successfully met the challenge.

Example: Helen Keller's Challenge

I had a difficult challenge in my life. When I was very young, I became deaf and blind. At first I couldn't speak. Finally Annie Sullivan became my teacher. She taught me sign language. I learned how to read, write, and even speak. I later went to college and wrote books.

Your Paragraph:

_____

_____

_____

_____

Unit 16

Travels in Laos

A. INTRODUCTION

1. On which continent is Laos? Name two countries that border on Laos.

2. Which two of the following statements are true about Laos?
    a. Laos has mountains, valleys, rivers, and jungles.
    b. Families are close in Laos, and as many as four generations live under one roof.
    c. Most Laotians speak both Laotian and Russian.

3. What are some things a tourist might do during a vacation in a foreign country? What would he/she talk about with other tourists?

UNIT 16

B. READING ACTIVITY

In this reading, Roger describes his travels in Laos.

1. **Reading Selection:** Travels in Laos

   Roger is a college student. He has been visiting Laos. He is talking with Ann, an American tourist. She has just arrived in Laos. She has seen nothing of the country so far.

   Ann: How long have you been in Laos?

   Roger: I've been here for about two months. I'm going back to the university next week.

   Ann: Have you enjoyed your stay in Laos?

   Roger: Yes, it's a fascinating place.

   Ann: Have you noticed the monsoons?

   Roger: I sure have. It is now the wet season. Now the monsoons are bringing rain and warm air.

   Ann: What interesting place have you visited?

   Roger: I saw the Plain of Jars. It's a grassy plateau that has more than a hundred large stone jars The jars are hundreds of years old. No one knows the purpose of the jars.

   Ann: Have you traveled to the capital yet?

   Roger: Yes, I have. I went to the city of Vientiane. It's a busy place. I saw the temple of Wat Sisaket with the thousands of miniature Buddhas inside.

   Ann: Have you been to a Laotian festival?

   Roger: Yes. I saw Boun, the festival after Buddhist Lent. There were actors doing shows during the festival. Some people were whispering a wish to a stone Buddha. They say if you can lift the Buddha, you will have your wish.

   Ann: Have you bought any Laotian crafts?

   Roger: Yes, I've bought several items. I have some baskets, handmade jewelry, and special cloth.

   Ann: Have you seen any wild animals?

   Roger: No, I haven't. I'd like to. I know there are leopards, tigers, and crocodiles in the jungle near the Mekong River.

   Ann: Have you traveled alone?

   Roger: Not all the time. My friend Gary was with me for a month. He went with me to the city of Vientiane and to the Plain of Jars. I can't wait to see everything here in Laos!

Glossary

miniature very small

monsoon a seasonal wind

plateau an elevated table of land.

2. **Comprehension Check**

Answer the following questions about the reading selection.

a. What is the weather like in Laos now?

b. Where has Roger traveled?

c. What festival did Roger see? Describe it.

d. What is unusual about the Plain of Jars?

e. Which place in Laos would you like to visit?

C. LISTENING ACTIVITY

1. **Prelistening**

You are going to hear more information about Laos. You will learn about the city of Vientiane, a special festival called Boun, the seasonal winds called monsoons, the Plain of Jars, and the Mekong River. Do you know anything about any of these topics?

2. **Listening**

First listen to the conversation about Laos. Then draw a line to match each topic from the conversation with the correct description.

Topics	Descriptions
a. Plain of Jars	1. They bring warm humid air and rain in May through October.
b. Vientiane	2. They are a mystery. There is a story that a prince brought them full of liquor to the plain. He wanted to celebrate a victory.
c. Boun festival	3. All major cities are on it.
d. Mekong River	4. It has many good high schools and the university.
e. monsoons	5. People tell the future using sticks at this event.

3. **Postlistening**

Is there a place in Laos or one of their customs that is similar to a place or custom in your country? What place or custom is most different from what you have in your country?

D. GRAMMAR

1. Grammar Explanation
Study the information and examples below.

Present Perfect Tense

Use the present perfect tense to talk about an action that began in the past and continues until the present.

FORM: "have" or "has" + (not) + main verb (past participle form)

Notes: 1. Use "have" or "has" in agreement with the subject.
2. The past participle for regular verbs is formed by adding "-ed" or "-d" to the base form of the verb.

Examples:

Questions	Answers
Have you visited Laos?	Yes, I've visited Laos.
Have you seen wild animals.	No, I haven't seen them.
Has he bought any crafts?	Yes, he has. He has bought some baskets.

Some irregular past participles:

base	past participle	base	past participle	base	past participle
be	been	have	had	buy	bought
make	made	come	come	see	seen
give	given	take	taken	go	gone
		write	written		

2. Grammar Practice
First change the base form of the verb to the present perfect and make a question. Then answer the question according to the information in the reading selection.

Example: Has Roger (be) to Laos?   Has Roger *been* to Laos?
Yes, he has. OR *Yes, Roger has been to Laos.*

a. Has Roger (enjoy) his visit to Laos? _____

b. Has Roger (be) in a monsoon? _____

c. Have Roger and Gary (see) the Plain Jars? _____

d. Have Roger and Gary (travel) to Vientiane? _____

e. Has Roger (be) to a festival? _____

f. Has Roger (buy) any Laotian crafts? _____

g. Has Roger (see) any wild animals? _____

h. Have you (visit) Laos? _____

E. SPEAKING

Ask a partner the following questions. Then change roles.

1. Have you been to the mountains?
2. Have you seen a river?
3. Have you traveled on a boat?
4. Have you been to a special festival?
5. Have you visited a zoo?

F. LANGUAGE

1. Language Explanation
Read the information about confusing words below.

> **Confusing Words: "it's" and "its"**
>
> People sometimes confuse "it's" and "its" and make mistakes using them.
>
> 1. "it's" = "it" + "is"
>   **Examples:** *It's time to go.*
>   *It's hot today.*
>
> "its" is a possessive pronoun. It comes before a noun to show possession.
>
> **Examples:** *The house had its lights on.*
> *She bought a used book. Its cover was missing.*

2. Language Practice
Choose "it's" or "its" to complete the blanks in the following sentences.

a. Laos has _____ flag on the state buildings.

b. I went to the Plain Jars. _____ a plateau with hundreds of jars.

c. _____ very hot during the summer in Laos.

d. I saw the capital. _____ very busy.

e. The baby dropped _____ food.

f. _____ a fascinating place.

g. _____ time to go back to the university.

UNIT 16

G. CHECK YOUR UNDERSTANDING

First write five sentences using "its" or "it's." Leave blanks for "its" or "it's." Then give the sentences to a partner to complete.

Example: *a fun festival.*

1. _____
2. _____
3. _____
4. _____
5. _____

H. CHECK YOUR PROGRESS

Rewrite the sentences and correct the errors. Look for three errors with the present perfect tense, two errors with "its" or "it's," and one spelling error. There is *one* error in each sentence.

> Gary and Roger have be to many places in Laos. They have saw the cities and the jungles. They has traveled on the Mekong River. Its hot during the summer, often over 100 degrees. They whent to the Bolovens Plateau. The Plateau is famous for it's pineapples and strawberries.

Example: Gary and Roger *have been* to many places in Laos.

_____
_____
_____
_____
_____

UNIT 16

I. WRITING FOR YOUR PORTFOLIO

Write a letter to someone about what you have done during the past month. Use the present perfect tense.

Example:

Dear Gloria,

How are you? I hope you're fine. I've had a great month. My friends and I have been to lots of parties. We've seen two movies. Both of the movies were funny. I've been on a diet. I've already lost five pounds. What have you done this month?

Yours,

Andrea

Your Letter:

_____

_____

_____

_____

Unit 17

The Panama Canal

A. INTRODUCTION

1. Which oceans border on Panama? Name two countries that border on Panama.
2. Which two of the following statements are true about Panama?
    a. It is against the law to sing or dance in Panama.
    b. Many of the people of Panama are a mixture of Indian groups with descendants of Spanish settlers.
    c. The climate is constant through the year, with high temperatures along the coasts between 85 and 90 degrees F.
3. Would you like to travel through the Panama Canal? Why?

B. READING ACTIVITY

This reading is about the Panama Canal, the passage between the Pacific and the Atlantic Oceans.

1. **Reading Selection:** Panama Canal

   One of the most famous places in Panama is the Panama Canal. This canal is a waterway between the Pacific and the Atlantic Oceans. Building the canal was very difficult. The canal is one of the greatest feats of the modern age.

   The length of the canal is 40 miles from coast to coast. There are six pairs of locks in the canal. These locks raise and lower the water level. That way the ships go up 85 feet above sea level, then back down to sea level. Taking the canal from the Atlantic to the Pacific makes the trip 7000 miles shorter.

   Even in the 1500s, people thought about a canal. In the 1800s, people made plans for a canal. Finally in 1906, work on the canal began. The United States made a treaty with Panama. The United States controlled the building of the canal. The U.S. also agreed to pay yearly rent to use the canal. Builders worked on the canal for 10 years, beginning in 1904. There were many problems. One big problem was disease. Yellow fever and malaria killed many workers. Fighting the war against disease was important to Dr. William Gorgas. He saved thousands of lives because of his work.

   In 1914, the first ship passed through the Panama Canal. Today ships pay about $30,000 to pass through the locks of the canal. Some ships pay more. Going through the locks is cheaper than sailing around South America, though. There are still problems with the canal. Repairing the locks is very difficult. Sometimes the canal gets crowded.

   ### Glossary

feat remarkable action	**malaria** disease spread by mosquitoes	**treaty** formal agreement between countries
lock a section of the canal that is raised or lowered		

2. **Comprehension Check**
   Answer the following questions about the reading selection.
   a. What does the Panama Canal connect?
   b. What was one problem in building the canal?
   c. Why do ships take the Panama Canal, even though it is very expensive?

C. LISTENING ACTIVITY

1. Prelistening
You are going to learn more details about the building of the Panama Canal. Originally, France wanted to build the canal. What is your guess why France didn't finish the project?

2. Listening
First listen to information about the Panama Canal. Then, choose the sentences that are true according to the information you hear.

a. i. The Spanish first started to build a canal in 1780 in Panama.
    ii. The French first started to build a canal in 1881 in Panama.

b. i. There were problems because of malaria, yellow fever, and the workers.
    ii. There were problems because of malaria, yellow fever, and the difficult land.

c. i. The United States bought the interest to build the canal from France.
    ii. The United States bought the interest to build the canal from Spain.

d. i. President Theodore Roosevelt made an agreement with Panama about the canal.
    ii. President Franklin D. Roosevelt made an agreement with Panama about the canal.

e. i. The engineer who finished the project was George Washington Goethals.
    ii. The engineer who finished the project was Dr. William Gorgas.

f. i. The canal cost less than $300,000,000 to build.
    ii. The canal cost more than $300,000,000 to build.

3. Postlistening
Do you think it would cost more or less to build the canal today? Why?

D. GRAMMAR

1. Grammar Explanation
Study the information and examples below.

> **Gerunds**
>
> Gerunds are verb forms that are used as nouns in a sentence. Gerunds take a singular verb when they are subjects in a sentence. To form a gerund, add "-ing" to the base form of the verb.
>
> Examples: *Building* the canal was difficult.
> *Going* through the locks is cheaper.
> Workers don't like *repairing* the locks.

2. Grammar Practice
Complete the following sentences about the Panama Canal. Use the gerunds in the box below.

raising	fighting	lowering
building	sailing	repairing
going		planning

Example: _____ the canal took a long time. *Planning* the canal took a long time.

a. _____ the canal took 10 years.

b. _____ the war against disease was important to Dr. Gorgas.

c. _____ the locks and _____ the locks allows ships to go from sea level to 85 feet above sea level.

d. _____ through the locks is cheaper than _____ around South America.

e. _____ the locks is difficult.

E. SPEAKING:
Ask a partner the following questions. Then change roles.
1. Do you prefer swimming or running?
2. Do you like riding a bike or sailing?
3. Do you prefer watching a sport or taking part in it?
4. Is reading or listening to music more enjoyable for you?
5. Why is smoking bad for your health?

F. LANGUAGE

1. Language Explanation
Read the information about abbreviations below.

Abbreviations

Abbreviations are a short form of the word or phrase. Below are some common abbreviations and their meanings.

Examples:

in.—inch	*qt.—quart*	*hr.—hour*	*ft.—foot*
c.—cup	*mo.—month*	*yd.—yard*	*gal.—gallon*
yr.—year	*mi.—mile*	*m.—meter*	*sq. mi.—square mile*
l.—liter	*oz.—ounce*	*doz.—dozen*	*lb.—pound*
pt.—pint	*sec.—second*	*min.—minute*	

UNIT 17

2. Language Practice

a. Write the abbreviations for the following words.

Example: *gallon—gal*

1. second	3. pound	5. foot	7. year	9. cup
2. ounce	4. mile	6. meter	8. month	10. liter

b. Write the words for the following abbreviations

Example: *doz. dozen*

1. sq. mi. _____
2. min. _____
3. pt. _____
4. hr. _____
5. yr. _____

6. yd. _____
7. in. _____
8. qt. _____
9. gal. _____
10. mo. _____

G. CHECK YOUR UNDERSTANDING

Write three questions using abbreviations. Give them to a partner to answer.

Example: Question - *How many min. are in an hr.?*
Partner's Answer - *60 min.*

1. _____
2. _____
3. _____
4. _____

H. CHECK YOUR PROGRESS

Rewrite the sentences and correct the errors. Look for two errors with gerunds, two errors with abbreviations, and two errors with capitalization. There is *one* error in each sentence.

> Going through the Panama Canal are very desirable. Many Ships save a lot of time by passing through the canal. Watched the locks raise and lower the ships is fun. Each lock is 1000 ftt. long. Almost 12,000 ships travel 40 mil. through the canal every year. Countries that use the canal include Japan, the United states, Great Britain, and Ecuador.

Example: Going through the Panama Canal *is* very desirable.

I. WRITING FOR YOUR PORTFOLIO

Write an essay about your activities during the weekend. Use two or more gerunds in your essay.

Example: My Weekend

During the weekend I like doing lots of activities. Saturday morning I like to go shopping with my friends. In the afternoon during summer I go swimming at the lake. In the evening I like to go dancing at parties or my friend's house. Sunday is a time for relaxing.

Your Paragraph:

Unit 18

Life in Antarctica

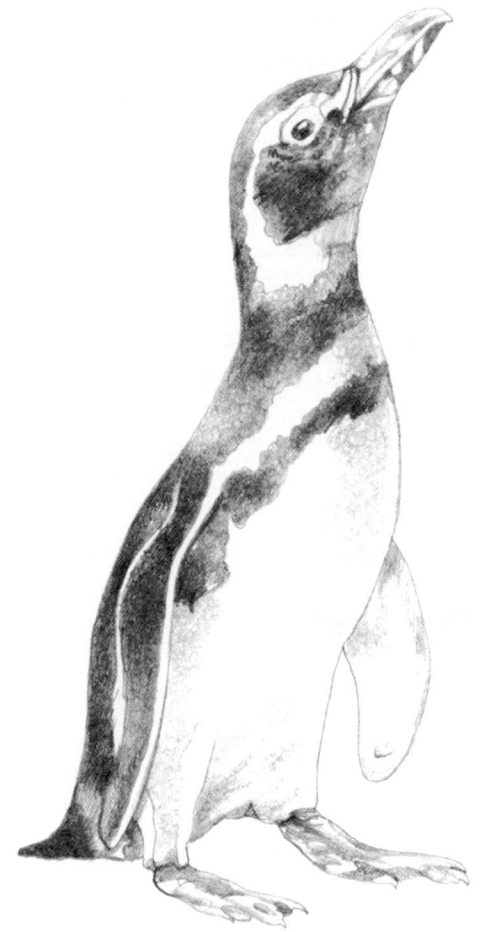

A. INTRODUCTION

1. Is Antarctica a country or a continent? Name the oceans that border on Antarctica.

2. Which two of the following statements are true about Antarctica?
   a. Antarctica exports products such as wheat and oranges.
   b. Antarctica is the coldest continent.
   c. Antarctica has no permanent human population.

3. What animal life do you think lives in the area of Antarctica?

B. READING ACTIVITY

This reading tells of animal and plant life on Antarctica.

1. Reading Selection: Life in Antarctica

Antarctica isn't the territory of any single country. Mainly twelve countries do research on this cold continent. These countries are Argentina, Australia, Chile, France, New Zealand, Norway, the United Kingdom, Belgium, Japan, South Africa, Russia, and the United States. These countries signed a treaty. It says that Antarctica is for peaceful purposes only.

The land in Antarctica has very little life. The cold and wind are too severe. There are some mosses and floating plants, and some mites. Scientists found bacteria growing just 183 miles from the South Pole or Antarctica. There is much more life in the sea. These sea animals spend most of the time in or over the water. The animals come on land only to breed. They have found 45 kinds of birds in Antarctica. Almost 80% of the birds in Antarctica are penguins. Penguins are excellent swimmers. They catch their food in the water. The emperor penguin is well known. Emperor penguins spend much of their life in the sea but lay their eggs and raise their young on land.

Another sea animal is the seal. The Weddell seal can dive as deep as 2,000 feet. Whales are also seen in the area. For example, schools of killer whales swim near the coasts of Antarctica. Fish such as the Antarctic cod and ice fish live in the waters of Antarctica. Fish in Antarctica have blood that lets them live in very cold water.

A very important part of the animal life in Antarctica is the krill. This creature looks like a small shrimp. Krill eat small marine plants and animals. They exist in large numbers. There may be as many as 5 billion tons of krill in Antarctica. Birds, seals, and whales eat krill.

Glossary		
breed to produce young	**mite** small animal related to the spider	**moss** small, green plant

2. Comprehension Check

Answer the following questions about the reading selection.

　　a. What do countries do in Antarctica?

　　b. What plants live on the land in Antarctica?

　　c. What animals live in the water in Antarctica?

UNIT 18

C. LISTENING ACTIVITY

1. Prelistening
You are going to listen to more information about wildlife in Antarctica. Some of the information you will hear is about the habitat of certain animals. The habitat is the place where animals live. Where do you think penguins, seals, and whales live most of the time?

2. Listening
First listen to more information on life in Antarctica. Then complete the chart below.

	Food	Habitat	Unusual feature
Emperor penguin			
Weddel seal			
Killer whale			

3. Postlistening
What do the penguin, seal, and whale have in common? How are they different?

D. GRAMMAR

1. Grammar Explanation
Study the information and examples below.

Passive Voice: Simple Present Tense

In the active voice, the subject does the acting. In the passive voice, the subject is acted upon by something or someone. To form the passive voice in the present tense, use the verb "to be" in the present tense and add the past participle form of the main verb.

Examples: ACTIVE - *Scientists find seals in Antarctica.*
PASSIVE - *Seals are found in Antarctica by scientists.*

---

2. Grammar Practice
First change the verb in parentheses to the simple present tense passive voice and rewrite the sentence. Use the past participles listed below to form the passive voice. Then, mark the sentences true (**T**) or false (**F**) according to the information in the reading selection.

Base Verb   **Past Participle**
    eat   eaten
    find   found
    govern   governed
    see   seen
    spend   spent
    use   used

Example: Seals, whales, and birds (find) in Antarctica.
Seals, whales, and birds *are found* in Antarctica. (**T**)

UNIT 18

1. Antarctica (govern) by Russia.

   _____ ( )

2. Scientists from Argentina and the United States (find) in Antarctica.

   _____ ( )

3. According to the treaty, Antarctica (use) for peaceful purposes only.

   _____ ( )

4. Not much life (find) on land in Antarctica.

   _____ ( )

5. Bacteria (find) near the South Pole.

   _____ ( )

6. For sea animals, most of their time (spend) on land.

   _____ ( )

7. About 45 kinds of birds (see) in Antarctica.

   _____ ( )

8. Krill (eat) by birds, seals, and whales.

   _____ ( )

E. SPEAKING:

Ask a partner the following questions using the passive voice. (If you don't know the names of the plants or animals, describe them.) Then change roles.

1. What kinds of plants are found in your neighborhood?
2. What kinds of animals are found in your area?
3. What birds are seen in your area?
4. What animals do you like that are found at the zoo?
5. What food is eaten by penguins?

125

F. LANGUAGE

1. Language Explanation
Read the information about vocabulary in science below.

> **Vocabulary - Words from Science**
>
> Here are some specialized words used in science. They are used to describe the life of animals.
>
> **species** a group of animals that are much alike
>
> **breed** to produce young
>
> **endangered** in danger of dying out
>
> **nocturnal** active at night
>
> **predator** a hunter of another animal
>
> **migration** to move from one region to another at the change of season
>
> **habitat** the place where an animal normally lives
>
> **environment** the area that has an effect on the development of an animal
>
> **extinction** no longer existing
>
> **tracks** marks left behind by an animal
>
> **prey** an animal taken by another animal for food

2. Language Practice
Complete the paragraph below about animals in the Antarctica. Use some of the words from science in the box above.

There are several _____ of animals in Antarctica. The _____ is not easy for
                                     a   b

living because of the extreme cold. The emperor penguin swims in the water, but

goes to the land to _____ . The penguins are not _____ animals because they
                                 c   d

are active in the day, not the night. Hunters kill penguins, and this killing could lead to the

penguin's _____ some day. One of the penguin's _____ is the whale. The whale's
                  e   f

_____ is the ocean.
    g

G. CHECK YOUR UNDERSTANDING

Write four questions about penguins, using some of the words from science. Then trade papers with a partner and answer the questions.

1. _____
2. _____
3. _____
4. _____

H. CHECK YOUR PROGRESS

Rewrite the paragraph and correct the errors. Look for three errors with passive voice, two errors with colons, and one spelling error. There is *one* error in each sentence.

> Antarctica is use by many countries for scientific exploration. Some of these countries are: United States, Japan, and Australia. Roald Amundsen was the first persen to reach the South Pole in 1911. Scientists today like to study: the climate, the animal life, and the plant life. Few plants are find on Antarctica. Most of the birds that are saw are penguins.

Example: Antarctica is *used* by many countries for scientific exploration.

_____

_____

_____

_____

_____

UNIT 18

I. WRITING FOR YOUR PORTFOLIO

Research an animal you like and write a paragraph about that animal. Write facts about the animal such as the animal's habitat, food, habits, predators, environment, chances for extinction, and so on.

Example:

The habitat for the emperor penguin is the land and sea in Antarctica. They are excellent swimmers. They eat fish and krill. One predator of the emperor penguin is the whale. The emperor penguins live in a cold and windy environment.

Your Paragraph:

_____

_____

_____

_____

_____

Unit 19

Nzinga
Queen of Ndongo and Matamba

A. INTRODUCTION

1. On which continent is Angola? Name two countries that border on Angola.

2. Which two of the following statements are true about Angola?

   a. Angola has a tropical rain forest.
   b. People from the Bantu and Bushmen tribes live in Angola.
   c. Angola is the largest country in Africa.

3. What are the qualities of a good leader?

B. READING ACTIVITY

This reading is about Nzinga, an African Queen from the area of Angola.

1. Reading Selection: Nzinga, Queen of Ndongo and Matamba

Nzinga Mbande was an African queen during the 1600s in the area of Angola. She ruled her territory from the capital of Luanda. She also fought against the Portuguese. In the early 1600s, the Portuguese controlled part of the African coast. For many years they tried to control Angola. Many stories and legends are told about her in Africa.

Nzinga's father, the ruler of Ndongo kingdom, traded peacefully with the Portuguese at first. Then in 1581, war broke out. Her father was killed, and his oldest son Mbandi took power. Mbandi sent his sister Nzinga to negotiate with the Portuguese. Nzinga met with the Portuguese governor. She entered the governor's room with her musicians and many servants. Nzinga saw there was only the governor's chair in the room. She told one of her servants to drop to her hands and knees. Nzinga sat on the woman like a chair. Then Nzinga made a treaty with the governor. The treaty gave Nzinga's people the land taken by the Portuguese. In return, Nzinga promised to help control the Jaga people.

Mbandi, Nzinga's brother, died in 1623. Nzinga became the queen of the Ndongo people. She rebuilt her army. The Portuguese attacked, but Nzinga escaped capture. She continued to build her army. By 1630, she was also in control of the Matamba kingdom. She worked with the Dutch to drive out the Portuguese. She continued to make negotiations with the Portuguese. In the end she gave up part of her territory but remained an independent ruler. Before her death in 1663, Nzinga became a Catholic.

In all, Nzinga ruled her people for forty years. She was able to protect her people against outsiders for many years. She is still remembered as a symbol of independence in Angola.

Glossary

negotiations talks to make an agreement   **treaty** a formal agreement between nations
territory land

2. Comprehension Check
Answer the following questions about the reading selection.

   a. Where and when was Nzinga a ruler?
   b. Why did she use her servant woman as a chair?
   c. Why do you think there are stories and legends about Nzinga?

C. LISTENING ACTIVITY

1. **Prelistening**
   You are going to complete an outline with facts about Nzinga. An outline gives the main ideas and supporting details on a topic. The main ideas are marked by Roman numerals (I, II, III, etc.). Look at the outline below. What three main ideas are included in the outline? What do you already know about these three main ideas?

2. **Listening**
   First listen to the information about Nzinga. Then complete the blanks in the outline below.

   Nzinga
   I. Nzinga's birth
      A. Nzinga was born in _____
      B. She was one of _____ children.
      C. Her brother's name was _____

   II. Nzinga's father dies
      A. The oldest son, became the _____
      B. He was forced to live on an _____

   III. Treaty with Portuguese governor
      A. Portuguese governor wanted to make _____
      B. Mbandi sent _____ to negotiate
         1. Nzinga made a treaty _____
         2. Nzinga's people would help the Portuguese fight the _____
         3. Nzinga's people were returned some of their _____

3. **Postlistening**
   Nzinga made an important negotiation. Do you think it is easy or difficult to negotiate with someone? Explain.

D. GRAMMAR

1. **Grammar Explanation**
   Study the information and examples below.

   > **Passive Voice: Simple Past Tense**
   > In the active voice, the subject does the acting. In the passive voice, the subject is acted upon by something or someone. To form the passive voice in the past tense, use the verb "to be" in the past tense and add the past participle form of the main verb.
   >
   > **Examples:** ACTIVE - *People told stories about Nzinga.*
   > PASSIVE - *Stories were told about Nzinga.*

UNIT 19

2. Grammar Practice

First change the verb in parentheses to the simple past tense passive voice and rewrite the sentence. Use the past participles listed below to form the passive voice. Then, mark the sentences true (**T**) or false (**F**) according to the information in the reading selection.

Base Verb	Past Participle
kill	killed
make	made
return	returned
rule	ruled
send	sent
take	taken
tell	told

Example: Angola (rule) by Nzinga during the 1400s.
Angola *was ruled* by Nzinga during the 1400s. (**F**)

a. Many stories (tell) about Nzinga in Africa.

_____ ( )

b. In the early 1600s, a section of African coast (control) by the Portuguese.

_____ ( )

c. Nzinga's father (kill).

_____ ( )

d. The rule (take) by Nzinga's brother called Mbandi.

_____ ( )

e. Nzinga (send) to negotiate with the Dutch.

_____ ( )

f. A treaty (make) by Nzinga and the Portuguese.

_____ ( )

g. Nzinga's people (return) land by the Portuguese.

_____ ( )

h. Her people (rule) by Nzinga for less than twenty years.

_____ ( )

E. SPEAKING

Ask a partner the following questions. Then change roles.

1. When and where were you born?
2. What were you called when you were young?
3. What stories were told to you by your family?
4. What were you given for your birthday?

F. LANGUAGE

1. **Language Explanation**
   Read the information about confusing words below.

   > **Confusing Words: "then" and "than"**
   >
   > People sometimes confuse "then" and "than" and make mistakes using them.
   >
   > a. "then" is an adverb meaning "at that time." It answers the question "When?"
   >   **Example:** *Then the war started.*
   >
   > b. "than" is a conjunction. It is used with comparisons of two or more things.
   >   **Examples:** *Nzinga was younger than her brother.*

2. **Language Practice**
   First choose the correct word and then rewrite each sentence..

   Example: (Then) (Than) the Portuguese settled in Africa.
   Then the Portuguese settled in Africa.

   a. Nzinga's father traded peacefully at first, but (then) (than) a war broke out.

   b. (Then) (Than) the oldest son became the ruler of Ndongo.

   c. Mbandi was older (then) (than) his sister Nzinga.

   d. Nzinga first talked to her brother, (then) (than) went to see the Portuguese governor.

   e. (Then) (Than) Nzinga sat down on the servant like a chair.

   f. The new treaty was better (then) (than) the treaty made before.

   g. After her brother's death, Nzinga (then) (than) became queen of Ndongo.

   h. Nzinga was a stronger ruler (then) (than) her father and brother.

UNIT 19

G. CHECK YOUR UNDERSTANDING

Write four sentences, using "then" and "than." Leave a blank for "then" and "than." Then give the sentences to a partner to complete.

1. _____
2. _____
3. _____
4. _____

H. CHECK YOUR PROGRESS

Rewrite the paragraph and correct the errors. Look for three errors with passive voice, two errors with "then" or "than," and one spelling error. There is *one* error in each sentence.

> Angola was rule by Portugal for almost 500 years. War were declared against Portugal in 1961. This war lasted more then 14 years. Independence was declare in 1975. Agostinho Neto was the first presdent of Angola. Than he died in 1979, and Jose dos Santos became president.

Example: Angola *was ruled* by Portugal for almost 500 years.

I. WRITING FOR YOUR PORTFOLIO

Research a famous a person and write a short biography about that person. Explain why the person is famous.

Example: Nzinga, African Queen

Nzinga was an a African queen during the 1600s in the area of Angola. She was queen of the Ndongo and Matamba people. She helped make a treaty with the Portuguese governor. Later she built an army. Nzinga continued to make negotiations with the Portuguese. She was a ruler for forty years.

Your Paragraph:

Unit 20

The Pot of Gold

A. INTRODUCTION

1. On which continent is Moldova? Name two countries that border on Moldova.

2. Which two of the following statements are true about Moldova?
    a. Moldova was one of the countries in the former Soviet Union.
    b. There are many Russians and Ukrainians in Moldova.
    c. Moldova has a population of less than 1,000 people.

3. What words of advice have your parents given you that have helped you in your life?

B. READING ACTIVITY

This is a folk tale about a father and his three sons from the area of Moldova.

1. Reading Selection: The Pot of Gold

Once there was a father and his three sons. The father was hardworking and labored from morning until night. On the other hand, his three sons did not work at all. They were healthy but very lazy.

As the father worked in the field and in the garden, the sons sat in the sun. Sometimes they went to Dniester River to fish.

"Why don't you help your father?" asked the neighbors. The sons said that their father didn't need them. The father did everything very well.

The father grew old and sick. The field and garden were filled with weeds. The sons still did nothing.

"Sons, why do you do nothing? I worked hard all my life. Now it is your turn." The sons did nothing.

One evening the old man was on his death bed. "My sons, how will you live on your own? Well, let me tell you a secret. Over the years I saved money. There is a pot of gold buried near the house. I don't remember where. Find it and you'll be rich." The old man died.

After their father's death, the sons were sad. Finally the oldest son said, "We don't even have money for bread. Let's look for the treasure."

The brothers dug everywhere around the house, but found nothing. They dug in the field, too. They found no sign of a pot of gold. After all their work, the garden was perfect for planting.

"As the garden and field are ready, let's plant some grapevines." The sons planted the grapevines and cared for them. Later they had a good harvest.

The oldest brother said, "I think we found our father's treasure."

Glossary

grapevine plant for grapes	**harvest** the gathering and bringing in of a farm product	**weed** a useless or unwanted plant

2. Comprehension Check

Answer the following questions about the reading selection.

a. Why didn't the sons help their father?
b. What did they do instead?
c. Why did the sons dig in the garden and field?
d. What do you think the father's treasure was?

C. LISTENING ACTIVITY

1. Prelistening
The boys in the story learned to enjoy working in the garden. Do you like garden work? Why or why not?

2. Listening
Read the story again. Then listen to a few questions about the story and write the answers in the space provided.

a. _____

b. _____

c. _____

d. _____

e. _____

f. _____

g. _____

h. _____

i. _____

j. _____

3. Postlistening
What is the message in this story? How did the three boys learn this important lesson?

D. GRAMMAR

1. Grammar Explanation
Study the information and examples below.

> **Reported Speech**
> Reported speech is a statement of what someone says or said in direct speech. The past tense is usually used in reported speech. The word "that" is optional in a sentence with reported speech. Be careful with the changes in pronouns!
>
> **Examples:**
>
> **DIRECT SPEECH -** The neighbors said, "The sons need to help their father."
> **REPORTED SPEECH -** The neighbors said (that) the sons needed to help their father.
> **DIRECT SPEECH -** The sons said, "Our father doesn't need our help."
> **REPORTED SPEECH -** The sons said (that) their father didn't need their help.

2. Language Practice

Change the sentences from direct speech to reported speech.

Example: The father said, "I like to work in the garden."
The father said *that he liked* to work in the garden.

a. The neighbors said, "The father works too hard." _____

b. The neighbors said, "The sons need to help their father." _____

c. The sons said, "Our father doesn't need our help." _____

d. The father said, "It is the sons' turn to work." _____

e. The father said, "I buried treasure in the garden." _____

f. The oldest son said, "We don't even have money for bread." _____

g. The sons said, "We will plant grapevines in the garden and field." _____

h. The oldest son said, "We have found our father's treasure." _____

E. SPEAKING

Ask a partner to answer the following questions using reported speech. Then change roles.

Example: What did your teacher say today?
The teacher said that he wanted everyone to read the book.

1. What did your teacher say today?
2. What did your friend say today?
3. What did your friend say to you last week?
4. What did you say to your family this morning?

F. LANGUAGE

1. Language Explanation
Read the information about punctuation below.

Punctuation – Quotation Marks

Use quotation marks to show someone's exact words – their direct speech. Use a comma after "said" when it introduces the quotation. Periods and commas go inside the quotation mark. The first letter in the quotation is capitalized.

Examples: *The oldest son said, "Let's go to the river."*
The neighbor said, "The sons don't help their father."
The oldest son said, "We don't even have money for bread."

2. Language Practice

Put the correct punctuation and capitalization in the following sentences.

Example: The father said I'm going to work in the garden.
The father said, "I'm going to work in the garden."

a. The son said let's go fishing in the river. _____

b. The neighbors said help your father in the fields. _____

c. The oldest son said I don't want to work. _____

d. The brother said let's go fishing at the river. _____

e. The old man said my sons let me tell you a secret. _____

f. The oldest son said let's look for the treasure. _____

g. The brother said let's dig the garden and the field. _____

h. The oldest brother said we found our treasure. _____

G. CHECK YOUR UNDERSTANDING

First listen to your partner talk about his or her weekend and write what he/she says using reported speech. Write four or more lines in total. Then change roles. Now tell a second partner what your first partner said and listen to what your second partner tells you.

Example: *Alex said that on Saturday he relaxed at home all day.*

_____

_____

_____

_____

_____

UNIT 20

H. CHECK YOUR PROGRESS

Rewrite the paragraph and correct the errors. Look for three errors in reported speech, two errors with quotation marks, and one error in spelling. There is *one* error in each sentence.

> Ivan said that his parents are born in Moldova. He say that before 1991, the area was called the Moldavian Soviet Socialist Republic. He also said that Moldova joins the Commonwealth of Independent States. Mary also had infomation about Moldova. Mary said "Moldova's economy is mostly agricultural." Ivan said, "My father's family grew grapes and different vegetables.

Example: Ivan said that his parents *were* born in Moldova.

I. WRITING FOR YOUR PORTFOLIO

Write a conversation between two speakers and discuss career interests. Use quotation marks. Write more than one quote for each speaker.

Example: Career Talk

Alex said, "I plan to be an engineer. I know that it takes a lot of studying for this career. I need to get excellent grades in math and go four years to a university."

Mary said, "I like the field of accounting. I'm good with numbers and I'm organized. I'll need to go to college, also."

Your Conversation:

Listening Scripts

Unit 1 – The Butchart Gardens

Mike: What is your favorite place to *visit*?
                                              a

Brandi I love to visit the Butchart Gardens. That place is just *beautiful*!
                                                                        b

Mike: Is it far?

Brandi: No. The gardens *aren't* very far. They are four *hours* from my house.
                             c   d

Mike: When do you go?

Brandi: I go all year long. There are cherry trees and daisies in the *spring*. In the
                                                                           e

summer there are *roses*. Also at night there are *fireworks*. In the *fall* I like the
                  f   g   h

colors of the trees. At Christmas time there are *special* lights and music.
                                                  i

Mike: Hey, now I'm *interested* in the gardens. Can I go *with* you sometime?
                       j   k

Brandi: *Sure*!
             l

Unit 2 – Sculptures in Stone

The Shona people in Zimbabwe are famous for their sculptures. The tradition of sculpture started long ago. The early Shona made sculptures 1,000 years ago. They made large birds of green stone on top of their buildings. Today some of these stone birds are in a museum.

Unit 3 – The Festival of Loi Krathong

a. Children ages 6-15 must go to school.

b. There is 1 television per 17 persons.

c. There is 1 telephone per 17 persons.

d. Men are expected to live until age 65.

e. Women are expected to live until age 73.

Listening Scripts

Unit 4 – The Boy Who Took Care of Pigs

    a. Who is the boy in the story?

    b. How old is the boy?

    c. Why can't the father work?

    d. What is Juanito's work?

    e. Where does Juanito take the pigs?

    f. Where does Juanito take the special wood?

    g. What really are the special sticks?

    h. What happens to the sticks of silver?

    i. What do Juanito and his parents build?

    j. Who do they invite to eat with them?

Unit 5 – Basanth The First Day of Spring

It's Basanth, a national holiday in Pakistan. Mohammed really enjoys this holiday. He is flying his Punjabi kite. His kite is high in the sky and is dancing in the wind. A small boy on top of a building is flying a kite. A tall, thin boy is trying to cut the string on Mohammed's kite. Alex, Mohammed's friend, is having fun. He is watching the contest from the street. Two girls are watching the contest from their window. They are cheering loudly. Mohammed's younger brother is named Abdul. He is standing next to Mohammed. The people are yelling and cheering for the kite competitors.

Unit 6 – The Gauchos

Argentina is famous for the tango. This dance started in the early 1900s. The dancers use long steps. The tango is also a song. These songs are usually sad stories. Sometimes tango dancers wear the clothes of the gaucho. Today people dance the tango all over the world.

Unit 7 – The Mouse Bride

    a. How many sons did Pekka have?

    b. What was the name of the youngest son?

    c. What were the three sons looking for?

    d. Where was Jukka walking?

    e. What did Jukka find in the tiny house?

    f. Does the mouse want to marry Jukka?

    g. Did all three brothers find brides?

    h. When are the brothers going to marry?

    i. What did the big boy do to the mouse and carriage?

    j. Who is the mouse bride really?

Listening Scripts

Unit 8 – The Lion and the Hare

<Use the same tone of voice for each character. The students should know through language, not voices>.

   a. "I plan to eat one of you every day."

   b. "We must make a plan. We're so afraid of being attacked."

   c. "Don't worry any longer. I have a plan to save both myself and all of you."

   d. "Hmmm. This well gives me an idea. I can see myself reflected in the water."

   e. "I will kill this other lion. I am the chief!"

   f. "Thank you so much! You rescued us!"

Unit 9 – Manatees

Here are some comparisons between manatees and other sea mammals, such as seals, walruses, and whales.

   a. Manatees are large and are heavier than seals.

   b. Whales are larger than manatees. Whales weigh 15 times as much as manatees.

   c. Whales are also more powerful than manatees.

   d. Manatees weigh more and in general are bigger than seals.

   e. Walruses weigh more than manatees, but manatees are longer than walruses.

   f. Seals swim faster than manatees; in comparison, manatees are rather slow.

   g. Manatees have offspring every two to three years, while seals have offspring every year.

   h. Only Eskimos may legally kill walruses. Even so, manatees are more endangered than are walruses.

Unit 10 – Three Major Cities

Ana: Which city do you like best – Chicago, New York City, or Los Angeles?

George: I like Los Angeles the best. L.A. has the most entertaining places, like the television studios.

Ana: I like New York City the best. They have the most interesting museums. They also have the most famous baseball team.

George: Los Angeles has the most relaxing weather. You don't have to worry about snow. You can also have fun outside all year around.

Ana: But New York City has the most wonderful places to visit. You can see the Empire State Building and the Statue of Liberty there.

Listening Scripts

Unit 11 – The Sahara Desert

Algeria is on the north coast of Africa. It is the second largest country in Africa. Part of Algeria is covered with the Sahara desert. This desert area has less than one inch of rain a year. Roads now cross the desert. Sometimes sand covers the road. Most Algerians live in the farm lands and cities in the north. The people mostly speak Arabic. The Muslim religion is the official religion.

Unit 12 – The Snow Woman

a. How did the woodcutter get money?

b. Why did the two woodcutters sleep in the hut?

c. What happened to the old man in the hut?

d. Why didn't the snow woman kill the young woodcutter?

e. What warning did the snow woman give to the young woodcutter?

f. Who came to the village a year later?

g. Did the woodcutter and Yuke have a family?

h. Why did the woodcutter tell Yuke his story?

i. What did the snow woman tell her husband?

j. What can you hear in the wind during a storm?

Unit 13 – Pablo Picasso

a. This is a 20th century movement in art. This art style expresses feelings and emotions. Expressionist painters liked strong colors and simple forms.

b. This is an artistic period during Picasso's life. He used many shades of blue in his paintings.

c. This is an artistic period during Picasso's life. He used many shades of red and rose in his paintings.

d. A modern art style created by Picasso and others between 1907 and 1914. Cubist pictures showed different sides of objects all at once. Painters used cubes and other geometric forms in their art.

e. This is a 20th century movement in art. Most important are colors and lines. Pictures are abstract and not realistic.

Unit 14 – The Widow and the Fish

a. She spent 35% of her money on food.

b. She spent 5% of her money on a new bed.

c. She spent 25% of her money on new clothes.

d. She spent 15% of her money on wood for the fire.

e. She gave 20% of her money to poor people.

Unit 15 – Helen Keller

Eighteen months after Helen Keller was born, she had a serious illness. She became deaf and blind. Helen's parents took her to see Alexander Graham Bell. Bell was the famous teacher of the deaf and inventor of the telephone. Through Bell, Annie Sullivan began to work with Helen in March, 1887. Annie Sullivan stayed with Helen as teacher and companion until Annie's death in 1936. At college, Helen used textbooks written in braille, a system of reading for blind people. During her life, Helen lectured in many different cities. She wrote several books about her life.

Unit 16 – Travels in Laos

Ann: Have you traveled to the Plain of Jars?

Roger: Yes, I have. The jars are a mystery. There is a story that a prince brought jars of liquor to the plain. He wanted to celebrate a victory.

Ann: Have you been to Vientiane?

Roger: Yes. The city has many good high schools and the university.

Ann: Have you seen the festival of Boun?

Roger: Yes, I have. There were people telling the future using sticks.

Ann: Have you seen the Mekong River?

Roger: Yes. All the major cities are on it.

Ann: Have you noticed the monsoons?

Roger: Yes. They bring warm humid air and rain in May through October.

Unit 17 – The Panama Canal

A French company first started to build a canal in Panama in 1881. There were problems because of malaria, yellow fever, and the difficult land. Work stopped in 1887. The United States bought the interests from France. President Theodore Roosevelt made an agreement to build the canal. The work on the canal began in 1904. George Washington Goethals, an engineer, finished the project. More than 40,000 workers built the canal. The canal cost $336,650,000 to make.

Unit 18 – Life in Antarctica

The emperor penguins eat fish for the most part. They nest on the ice and spend much of their time in the water. The emperor penguin females leave their eggs in order to feed. The male then sits on the eggs for two months.

Weddell seals eat food such as fish and birds. They live in the sea most of the year. They can dive as deep as 2000 feet and stay down for nearly an hour.

Killer whales eat penguins and seals. They live entirely in the water, mostly near the coast. They even attack other whales two or three times their size.

Unit 19 – Nzinga, Queen of Ndongo and Matamba

Nzinga was born in the 1600s. Her father was the ruler of the kingdom of Ndongo. Nzinga was one of five children. The oldest son became king after his father was killed. This son's name was Mbandi. Mbandi couldn't control the Portuguese. The ruler was forced to go live on an island. Problems continued. The Portuguese governor wanted to make peace. Mbandi sent his sister Nzinga to negotiate. Nzinga made a treaty with the governor. She said her people would help the Portuguese fight the Jaga people. The Jaga were a group of slaves and criminals. In return, Nzinga's people were given back some of their land.

Unit 20 – The Pot of Gold

    a. What country is this story from?

    b. What is the title of the story?

    c. What did the father do with his time?

    d. What did the three sons do with their time?

    e. Why didn't the sons help their father?

    f. What did the father tell his sons on his deathbed?

    g. Where did the sons look for the treasure?

    h. What did the sons do with the garden after the digging?

    i. What happened to the grapevines?

    j. Do you think the sons are happy with their "treasure"?